# THE TASTE OF ITALY

*Also available in Papermac*

The Taste of France

# THE TASTE OF ITALY

A dictionary of Italian food and wine

Fay Sharman and Brian Chadwick

First published 1985 by
PAPERMAC
a division of Macmillan Publishers Limited
4 Little Essex Street London WC2R 3LF
and Basingstoke

Associated companies in Auckland, Delhi, Dublin, Gaborone, Hamburg, Harare, Hong Kong, Johannesburg, Kuala Lumpur, Lagos, Manzini, Melbourne, Mexico City, Nairobi, New York, Singapore and Tokyo

*British Library Cataloguing in Publication Data*

Sharman, Fay
The taste of Italy : a dictionary of Italian food and wine.
1. Cookery, Italian — Dictionaries
2. Beverages — Italy — Dictionaries
I. Title II. Chadwick, Brian
641′.0945 TX723

ISBN 0-333-37575-0

Printed and bound in Great Britain by
Redwood Burn Limited, Trowbridge, Wiltshire

*Introduction*

This dictionary is designed to take the guesswork out of identifying and enjoying Italian food and wine, wherever it may be found. It is a companion guide to restaurant eating, written especially for those visiting Italy, and will be a handy reference too when shopping.

The book gives simple non-technical definitions in English of words likely to be encountered on an Italian menu. It is arranged in alphabetical order, with cross reference to separate entries indicated by the use of italics. *The Taste of Italy* is *not* an encyclopaedia, nor can it do justice to the great diversity of Italian food and wine. In this respect Italy remains very much a geographical experession and, quite apart from obvious contrasts between north and south, each region – each town, even – has its own distinctive culinary tradition. Language differences further complicate the picture, although we have included dialect translations where appropriate. However, it is fair to warn the reader that Italian spelling is often erratic, while the habit of finishing words with a diminutive '-etto' or '-ino' may be significant or merely a flourish.

Restaurants in Italy do not always provide menus and wine lists are rarer still. Our coverage of the vast subject of Italian wines is, of necessity, restricted to those classified as DOC, but we have also managed to mention many good wines which fall outside the official ratings. We recommend the works of Burton Anderson and Victor Hazan for amplification.

We would like to thank Gordon Brown and the Italian Trade Centre for advice.

Fay Sharman and Brian Chadwick
March 1985

Regional capitals
Bolzano
VALLE D'AOSTA
Aosta
TRENTINO ALTO ADIGE
Trento
FRIULI VENEZIA GUILIA
Trieste
Milan
LOMBARDIA
VENETO
Venice
Turin
PIEMONTE
EMILIA ROMAGNA
Bologna
LIGURIA
Genoa
SAN MARINO
Florence
TOSCANA
MARCHE
Ancona
Perugia
UMBRIA
L'Aquila
ABRUZZO
MOLISE
Rome
LAZIO
Campobasso
Bari
PUGLIA
CAMPANIA
Naples
BASILICATA
Potenza
SARDEGNA
Cagliari
CALABRIA
Catanzaro
Palermo
SICILIA

## Abbacchio
(Lazio) Baby milk-fed lamb. *A. alla cacciatora*: pot roasted with wine, herbs, anchovies and hot pepper.

## Abbaia
(Sardegna) Strong red wine made by the Vermentino cooperative, for drinking young.

## Abboccato
Palatable. Slightly sweet, of wines.

## Abbote
(Lazio) Variety of *mozzarella* cheese.

## Abbrustolito
Toasted.

## (All') Abruzzese
In the style of *Abruzzo*. With hot red pepper. See also *arrosticini, cannochie, cassata, cosciotto, fagioli, polpo, timballo, triglie*.

## Abruzzo
*DOC* region producing red and white wines based on *Montepulciano*and *Trebbiano* grapes.

## A'bubbedella
(Campania) Pasta and vegetable soup.

## Accartocciato
Twisted, wrapped.

## Accia
(Campania) Celery.

## Acciughe
Anchovies. *A. all'arancia* (Sicilia): baked with lemon, olives, pine nuts and orange juice. *A. alla carabiniera*: with potato salad. *A. contadina*: in salad, with capers, onions, olives. *A. ripiene* (Liguria): stuffed with herbs cheese and eggs, deep fried.

## Accomodato
See *stoccafisso*.

## Aceto
Vinegar. *A. balsamico*: aged sweet-sour vinegar; the most famous and expensive, at least 10 years old, is produced in Modena and often sold as 'aceto del duca', after the dukes of Modena.

## Acetini
Gherkins, pickles.

## Acetosa
Sorrel, the vegetable.

## Acido
Acid, pickled.

**Acini**
Pips. *A. d'uva*: grapes.
Tiny pasta shapes, for soups.

**Acqua**
Water.

**Acquacotta**
(Toscana, Umbria) Vegetable soup, simple or elaborate, poured over slices of bread; also known as *zuppa alla grossetana*.

**Acquavite**
Raw distilled spirit.

**Acqui**
(Piemonte) Small town making *DOC* wines, dry red from *Dolcetto* and sweet, sometimes sparkling, red from *Brachetto* grapes.

**(Alla moda dell') Adriatico**
Adriatic style. Grilled over wood or charcoal, of fish.

**Affettato**
Sliced ham or sausage.

**Affile**
(Lazio) Small town and its red *DOC* wine from *Cesanese* grapes, dry or sweet, or sparkling.

**Affogato**
Poached, steamed.

**Affumicato**
Smoked, cured.

## Aggiadda
(Liguria) Garlic sauce.

## Agio e ogio
(Veneto) Oil and garlic, as a dressing.

## Aglianico
Red grape variety grown in the south, producing big, dark strong wines.

## (All') Agliata
With garlic sauce. Garlic pounded with vinegar-soaked breadcrumbs.

## Aglio
Garlic. *Aglio e olio*: garlic and oil, a basic sauce for pasta.

## Agnello
Lamb. *Agnello pasquale*: spring, Easter, lamb. *A. a cacio e uova*(Abruzzo): stew, finished with beaten egg and cheese. *A. alla carbonara*: cooked in a pot lined with paper to absorb the fat. *A. a cutturo* (Abruzzo): stewed in a copper pot ('cutturo') with herbs and hot pepper, served with bread. *A. friulano*: stewed with vinegar and horseradish. *A. alla romagnola*: simmered in tomato sauce, with peas. *A. alla romana*: pieces rolled in breadcrumbs and herbs, baked. *A. in umido alla sarda: larded with herbs, stewed in oil and tomatoes.*
*Agnello pasquale*(Sicilia): sweet pastry stuffed with citron paste.

## Agnol(in)i
(Lombardia) Pasta squares or peaked caps stuffed with chicken, cheese, spices, served in chicken broth.

## Agnolotti/agnulot
(Piemonte) Rectangular or crescent-shaped pasta envelopes with a meat stuffing, served with meat sauce or melted butter; also known as *pazlache*.

## Agoni
Small flat freshwater fish, found especially in Lake Como and often salted and dried (*misoltini/missoltitt*). *A. alla comasca*: marinated and fried, with anchovy sauce.

## Agnostinelle
(Puglia, Abruzzo) Tiny red mullet, floured and fried.

## (Di) Agrigento
Of Agrigento, *Sicilia*. See *carciofi, cavolo, cuddiruni.*

## (All') Agro
Sour with lemon. Dressed with oil and lemon.

## Agrodolce
Sour-sweet. With a vinegar and sugar sauce, plus perhaps raisins, pine nuts, wine.

**Aguglia**
Garfish.

**Ajo e ojo**
(Lazio) Oil and garlic.

**Ajula**
(Sicilia) Striped sea bream.

**Alaccia**
Large type of sardine.

**Alalonga**
Albacore, type of tuna fish.

**(Alla moda d') Alba**
In the style of Alba, *Piemonte*. With truffles. See also *insalata, lasagne*.
Important wine town producing red *DOC* wines from *Barbera, Dolcetto* and *Nebbiolo*.

**Albana**
(Emiglia-Romagna) White grape variety.

**Albergo**
Hotel, inn.

**Albicocche**
Apricots.

**Alborella**
Freshwater fish.

**Alcamo**
(Sicilia) Light dry white *DOC* wine.

**Alce**
Elk.

**Alchermes**
Brandy-based liqueur, infused with spices and coloured red with cochineal.

**Aleatico**
Red grape variety grown mainly in the south, producing dark sweet dessert wines.

**Alette**
Wings, of chicken, turkey.

**Alezio**
(Puglia) Small town known for red and rosé *DOC* wines based on *Negroamaro* grapes.

**(All') Alfredo**
See *fettuccine*.

## Alici
Anchovies. *A. areganate/arracanate*(Campania, Puglia): baked with oil, garlic, breadcrumbs, capers, mint, oregano.

## Alimentari
Groceries. Grocer's store.

## All'/alla
In the style of. With.

## Allodole
Larks.

## Alloro
Bayleaves.

## Allungato
Diluted, 'long' of drinks.

## Al macc
(Piemonte) Rice with milk soup with chestnuts.

## Alosa
Shad, migratory fish. *Alose in camicia* (Sicilia): baked in pastry with hot peppers.

## Alto Adige
*DOC* zone for 16 wines, all named according to grape variety, labelled in Italian or German.

## (All') Altoatesina
In the style of *Alto Adige*. See *uova*.

## Amabile
Semi-sweet, of wines.

## Amarene
Morello cherries.

## Amaretto
Apricot or almond liqueur. *A. di Saronno* is considered the best.
*Amaretti*: Macaroons; made in great variety throughout Italy.
*Amarettus*: Sardinian version.

## Amaro
Bitter.
Pungent drink usually containing iron and quinine and sold with strong brand image, e.g. Ramazzotti, Montenegro, Unicum; said to have stimulative, digestive, tonic and even aphrodisiacal properties.

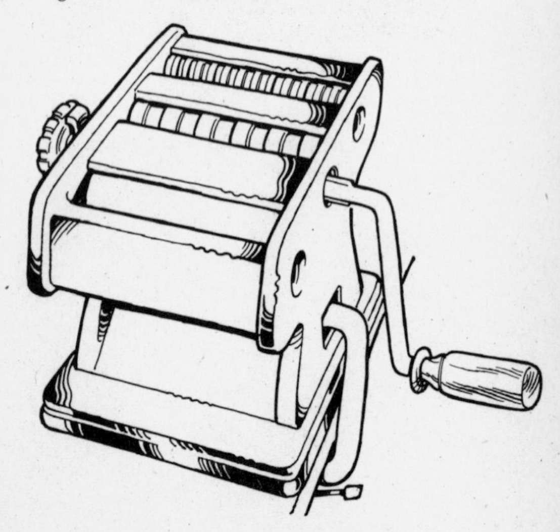

## Amarone
(Veneto) Strong, dark red, slightly bitter wines made from specially selected and semi-dried grapes. See also *Recioto*.

## (All') Amatriciana
In the style of Amatrice, *Lazio*. With a sauce of tomatoes, onions, pork jowl, hot pepper and perhaps white wine, especially of pasta, rice.

## (All') Ambrosiana
Ambrosial. See also *funghi*.

## (All') Amburghese
Hamburg-style. See *bistecca*.

**(Alla maniera d') Amelia**
In the style of Amelia, *Umbria*. See *colombo*.

**Americano**
American. Drink of half Campari, half sweet red vermouth.

**Ammantato**
'Blanketed'. Covered with another ingredient, perhaps cheese.

**(All') Ammiraglia**
'Admiral's style'. With seafood as an ingredient.

**Ammiru**
(Sicilia) Prawns.

**Ammiscato**
See *pasta*.

**Ammollicato**
Steeped, softened.

**(All') Anacaprese**
In the style of Anacapri, *Campania*. See *totano*.

**Analcolico**
Soft drink.

**Ananas(so)**
Pineapple.

**Ana(t)ra**
Duck. *A. col pien* (Veneto): stuffed with meat, sausage, mushrooms and pistachios, boiled.

**Ancidda**
(Sardegna) Eel.

**(All') Anconetana**
In the style of Ancona, *Marche*. See *brodetto, frittata, olive, pincinelle, stoccafisso*.

**(Alla maniera di) Andria**
In the style of Andria, *Puglia*. See *maccheroni, quaghiaridd*.

**Anello**
Dish in a ring shape, e.g. *anello di risotto*.
*Anellini*: tiny pasta rings, for soups.

**Anghelu Ruju**
(Sardegna) 'Red angel'. Heavy red dessert wine made by *Sella & Mosca*.

**Angiulottus**
See *culingiones*.

**Anguele in salsa**
(Veneto) Small fish fried and marinated in vinegar.

## Anguidda

(Sicilia) Eel

## Anguilla

Eel. *Anguille all' acqua di mare*(Puglia): baby eels covered in seawater and dried in the sun. *Anguilla all' aretina*: slices baked on skewers with bread slices and sage. *A. alla maniera di Cascia*: similar, with bayleaves. *A. alla moda del fattore*: crisp fried, with gherkins and mustard sauce. *A. alla fiorentina*: baked whole with herbs and red wine. *A. alla trentina*: marinated and fried, with cheese. *A. in umido*: stewed, with tomatoes, mushrooms, wine, etc. *A. alla veneziana*: with tuna and lemon.

## Anguria

Water melon.

## Anice

Aniseed. *A.stellato*: star anise.

## Animelle

Sweetbreads. *A. di agnello alla romana*: lamb's, with mushrooms and marsala. *A. di agnello alla trasteverina*: marinated and deep fried.

## Anitra

Duck. *A. farcita alla novarese*: boned, stuffed with veal, sausage, rice, roast and served with rice. *A. alla romagnola*: with bacon and wine. *A. selvatica fredda alla sarda*: cold boiled wild duck with myrtle.

## Annata

Year of vintage, of wine.

## Annegato

'Drowned'. Simmered in wine.

## Anolini

(Emilia-Romagna) Small pasta envelopes with a meat stuffing.

## (All') Antica

'Old style, old-fashioned, classic'. See also *piselli*.

## Antinori

Prominent family of *Chianti* producers

## Antipasto

Preliminary course of a meal, hors d'oeuvre, preceding the first course of soup or pasta. *Antipasti* often consist of pork products, fish, vegetables and salads and in a restaurant will be prominently displayed. *Antipasto alla genovese*: young broad beans with sausage and cheese. *A. di grasso*: mixed meats. *A. magro*: mixed vegetables and salads, perhaps tuna and hard boiled eggs. *A. pasquale*: usually sausage, eggs, radishes and celery. *A. quaresimale*: including fish, eggs, vegetables etc.

## (Di) Antrodoco

Of Antrodoco, *Lazio*. See *stracci*.

## Aole
Freshwater fish.

## Aperitivo
Aperitif.

## Aperol
Branded aperitif made by Barbieri.

## Apparecchiato
Prepared. See also *capone*.

## Aprilia
(Lazio) Small town producing red and white *DOC* wines from *Merlot, Sangiovese* and *Trebbiano* grapes.

## Aquileia
(Friuli-Venezia Giulia) *DOC* region for 7 wines named according to grape variety.

## (All') Aquilina
In the style of L'Aquila, *Abruzzo*. See *gravioli, sagnette*.

## Arachide
Peanut, groundnut.

## Aragosta
Langouste, rock lobster, crawfish. Popularly, lobster. *A. alla siciliana*: cooked in oil, with white wine, parsley, lemon.

*Aragosta* (Sardegna): dry white wine made from *Vermentino* grapes.

## Arancia/arancio
Orange. *A. cardinale* (Lazio): opened into segments and dressed with salt and olive oil.

**Aranciata**

Orangeade.

**Arancine**

'Little oranges'. (Sicilia) Veal and rice croquettes. *A. di magro*: rice balls with mushrooms, cheese and peas.

**Aranzada**

(Sardegna) Almond and honey sweetmeat.

**Arca di Noe**

Small shellfish.

**Areganato**

With oregano.

**(All') Aretina**

In the style of Arezzo, *Toscana*. See *anguilla, cosciotto, fagiolini, pollo*.

**Argentina**

Argentine, similar to sardine. See also *pesce*.

**(All') Argintera**

In the style of Argento, *Sicilia*. See *caciu*.

**Arigusta**

Crawfish.

**Aringhe**

Herring.

**Arista**

(Toscana) Loin of pork, roast or spit-roasted with herbs.

**Armleti**

(Tosana) Savoury dumplings.

**Arneis**
(Piemonte) White grape variety.

**Aromatizzato**
Aromatized, of wine. Wine with addition of herbs and spices, similar to vermouth.

**(All') Arrabbiata**
(Lazio) 'Rabid'. With hot red pepper sauce, of pasta, particularly *penne*.

**Arracanato**
With oregano.

**Arricchito**
Enriched, e.g. with cream.

**Arrosticini all' abruzzese**
Skewers of lamb grilled over charcoal.

**Arrostini**
(Lombardia, Piemonte) Chops, fillets of veal, typically cooked with white wine and sage.

**Arrosto**
Roasted, roast meat. Baked dish. *A. morto* (Toscana): veal, chicken, pigeon or similar roasted with oil and garlic. *A. segreto* (Marche): sardines and herbs baked in a covered ('secret') dish.

**Arrotolato**
Rolled up.

**Arselle**
(Liguria, Sardegna, Toscano) Small clams; or wedge shells.

**Articiocch**
(Lombardia) Artichokes.

**Arvier**
(Valle d'Aosta) Small town known for dry red *DOC* wine, *Enfer d'A.*

**Arzilla**
(Lazio) Skate, ray.

**Asciutto**
Dry. See also *minestra, pasta.*

**(All') Ascolana**
In the style of Ascoli, *Marche*. See *calcioni, capretto, olive.*

**Asiago**
(Veneto) Hard, granular, quite sharp cheese, made by farms.

**Asineddu**
(Sicilia) Picarel, sea fish.

## Asino
Donkey.

## Asparagi
Asparagus, often served with parmesan. *A. alla bassanese*: steamed, with spicy oil and lemon sauce. *A. alla fiorentina/alla milanese*: with parmesan and fried eggs.

## (Di) Assisi
Of Assisi, *Umbria*. See *rocciata*.

## Assonza
(Basilicata) Lard flavoured with hot pepper and fennel seeds, spread on toast.

## Assortito
Assorted.

## Astaco
Lobster.

## (All') Astesana
In the style of Asti, *Piemonte*. See *côtletta*.

## Asti
(Piemonte) Town and major *DOC* region, famous for the sparkling *A. spumante*, made from *Moscato* grapes by the Charmat method, produced and distributed mainly by large companies, e.g. *Martini & Rossi, Fontanafredda, Cinzano*. *Moscato naturale d'A.*: still sweet wine, mostly made into *A. spumante*. Varietal red wines are from *Barbera, Dolcetto, Freisa* and *Grignolino* grapes. *Malvasia di Casorzo d'A*: sweet lightly sparkling red wine.

## Astice
Lobster.

## Atterato
See *vermicelli*.

## Attorta
(Umbria) S-shaped almond cake.

## Aurum
(Abruzzo) Gold-coloured liqueur of oranges, herbs and brandy.

## Auslese
(Alto-Adige) Made from selected grapes, of wine.

## (All') Avellinese
In the style of Avellino, *Campania*. See *capretto*.

## Avellino
(Campania) Town known for distinguished dry white wine based on *Fiano* grapes.

## Avemarie
(Lazio) Small pasta tubes.

## Avvocato
Avocado pear.

## Azienda
Business, firm. *A. agricola*: farm. *A. vinicola*: winery. *A. viniviticola: wine estate and winery.*

## Babà
(Campania) Rum baba.

## (Alla) Babi
See *pollo.*

## Bacalà
(Veneto) Dried cod (*stoccafisso* not *baccalà*) stewed with onions and anchovies, finished with cheese, milk and oil.

## Baccalà
Dried salt cod. *B. alla bolognese*: stewed with oil, butter, garlic, parsley. *B. alla cappucina* (Veneto, Friuli): with anchovies, garlic, perhaps pine nuts, raisins, garlic, served with *polenta. B. alla fiorentina*: fried, with garlic and tomato sauce. *B. a ghiotta* (Sicilia): served with tomatoes, potatoes, pears, olives etc. *B. in guazzetto* (Lazio): fried, with tomato sauce, raisins, nuts. *B. mantecato* (Veneto): steamed, then pounded to a thick cream, eaten with sliced *polenta. B. al forno alla monticiana*: baked with tomatoes and herbs. *B. alla napoletana*: fried, with garlic, olives, capers, tomatoes. *B. alla trasteverina*: with anchovies, capers, pine nuts, raisins. *B. al verde* (Liguria): similar, plus potatoes. *B. alla vicentina*: stewed in milk with herbs, spices, anchovies, cheese, served with *polenta.*

## Bacche
Berries, fruit.

## Baci
(Liguria) Chocolate or lemon sweetmeats.
*Baci di dama* (Piemonte): almond biscuits.

## Badduzze
(Sicilia) Meat balls simmered in tomato sauce.

## Baggiana
(Umbria) Bean, tomato and basil soup.

## Bagna caoda/cauda
(Piemonte) Hot oil, anchovy and garlic dip, for raw vegetables, especially cardoons.

## Bagnet
(Piemonte) *B. 'd tômatiche*: tomato sauce. *B. verd*: garlicky green sauce. Both traditional with boiled meats.

## Bagnun de anciue
(Liguria) Anchovy and tomato soup.

## Bagoss/bagozzo
(Lombardia) Hard grainy cheese, sharp and aromatic.

## Baicoli
(Veneto) Small biscuits, dipped in sweet wine or hot chocolate.

## Baldonazzi
(Trentino-Alto Adige) Small sausages of pig's blood, raisins, chestnuts, sliced and fried.

## Bale d'asu
(Piemonte) Round boiling sausage.

## Balestra
See *pescè*.

## Ballot ed pôlenta
(Piemonte) Grilled or fried *polenta* and cheese croquettes.

## Balsamella
Béchamel sauce.

## Banana
Banana.
(Lombardia) Long soft bread roll.

## Barbabietole
Beetroot.

## Barbarcarlo
(Lombardia) Fine red *DOC* wine cased on *Barbera* grapes.

## Barbaresco
(Piemonte) Village renowned for red *DOCG* wine from the *Nebbiolo* grape, minimum 12.5° alcohol and 2 years ageing; widely distributed.

## (Alla) Barbaroux
See *cannelloni*.

## Barbera
(Piemonte) Widely grown grape variety, producing big dry red wines.

## Barbi
Small freshwater fish.

**Barchetta**
Boat shape, tartlet, barquette, of food.

**Bardele**
(Lombardia) Pasta ribbons. *B. coi marai*: made with borage leaves.

**Bardolino**
(Veneto) Small town famous for its light dry red *DOC* wines.

**(Alla) Barese**
In the style of Bari, *Puglia*. See *calamari, cappello da gendarme, cozze, orata, peperoni, pizzella*.

**Bargulle**
(Piemonte) Boiled chestnuts with milk, cream or white wine.

**Barile**
See *casereccio*.

**Barletta**
(Puglia) Coastal port making dry red *DOC* wine.

**Barolo**
(Piemonte) Village making one of Italy's finest red wines (*DOCG*), from *Nebbiolo*, with a minimum of 13° alcohol and 3 years ageing in wood; it may be called *riserva* after 4 years and *riserva speciale* after 5 years.

**Barzotte**
Soft-boiled, of eggs.

**Basilico**
Basil, the herb.

**(Alla) Bassanese**
In the style of Bassano del Grappa, *Veneto*. See *asparagi*.

**Bastoncini**
Stick-shaped biscuits.

**Batsoà**
(Piemonte) Pig's trotters, dipped in egg and breadcrumbs and fried; also known as *piedini di maiale alla piemontese*.

**Battelnatto**
(Piemonte) Type of cheese.

**Battuto**
Foundation, garnish for stew or soup, of onion and other vegetables, perhaps ham, browned in fat.

**(Alla) bava**
See *gnocchi*.

**Bavette**
(Liguria) Long thin pasta noodles, for soup.

## Bavose

Blenny, small sea fish used in soups.

## Beccaccia

Woodcock. *Beccacce alla norcina*: stuffed with the entrails, herbs and truffle, spit-roasted. *B. alla ternana*: served on fried bread spread with the entrails.

## Beccaccino

Snipe.

## Beccafichi

Figpeckers, small birds, usually grilled on skewers. *B. al nido*(Liguria): baked on large mushrooms. See also *sarde*.

## Beccute

(Marche) Maize flour cakes with pine nuts and sultanas.

## (A la) Bechèra

See *sguazeto*.

## (Alla) Bela Rosin

See *uove*.

## Bellini

Champagne with peach juice, a speciality of Harry's Bar in Venice. See also *spaghetti*.

### Bel Paese
(Lombardia) Soft creamy mild cheese, made by the Galbani firm who created it in the 1920s.

### Bensone
(Emilia-Romagna) Lemon flavoured bread, sometimes in a spindle shape.

### (Alla) Bergamasca
In the style of Bergamo, *Lombardia*. See *polenta*.

### Bergne
(Piemonte) Mutton hams.

### Berlingozzi
(Toscana) Sweet ring-shaped fritters.

### Berodo
(Liguria) Blood pudding.

### Bertani
Important producers of *Veneto* wines.

### Besciamella
Béchamel sauce.

### (Di) Bettona
Of Bettona, *Umbria*. See *zuccherini*.

### Bevanda
Drink.

## Bev'r in vin
(Lombardia) Bowl of meat broth with red wine.

## Bianchello
(Marche) White grape variety.

## Bianchetti
(Liguria) Tiny sardines or anchovies; also known as *gianchetti*.

## Bianco
White. Plainly boiled, of rice. *In bianco*: without tomatoes, of pizza, sauces.

*Bianco e nero* (Liguria): liver, brains, sweetbreads etc. breadcrumbed and fried; also known as *gianchi e neigro*.

(Calabria) Centre of *DOC*zone producing *Greco di B.*: light dry white table wine, or fine dessert wine made from semi-dried grapes; also known as *Greco di Gerace*.

## Bianco vergine Val di Chiana
(Toscana): Fine dry white *DOC* wine based on *Trebbiano* grapes.

## Biancolella
(Campania) White grape variety

## Bicciolani
(Piemonte) Sweet biscuits.

## Bieda
Beet, the vegetable.

## Bibita
Drink.

## (Alla) Biellese
In the style of Biella, *Piemonte*. See *tagliatelle*.

## Biete
Swiss chard, the vegetable.

## Bietole
Spinach beet.

## Bigarani
(Veneto) Sweet biscuits.

## Bignè
Fritters. *B. di San Giuseppe* (Lazio): small sweet fritters traditional on St Joseph's day.

(Lazio) Round bread roll.

## Bigoli
(Veneto) Thick homemade spaghetti. *B. con l'anara*: in duck broth with giblets. *B. col pocio*: with meat sauce. *B. in salsa*: with onions and anchovies.

### Biondi-Santi
Renowned producers of *Brunello di Montacino.*

### Biova
(Piemonte) Large round bread loaf. *Biovetta*: smaller version.

### Biroldo
(Toscana) Blood pudding, with pine nuts and raisins, or cheese.

### Birra
Beer. *B. estera*: foreign beer. *B. nazionale*: Italian beer. *B. alla spina*: draught beer. See also *pane.*

### Bisato
(Veneto) Eel. *B. in tecia*: slices fried and finished with wine and tomatoes served with *polenta. B. sull'ara*: baked with bayleaves,originally in the space ('ara') above the glass-making kiln.

### Biscione
(Emilia-Romagna) Almond pastry.

### Biscotti(ni)
Biscuits.

### Biscotto
Sponge cake.

### Biscuit tortone
Ice cream.

### Bisna
(Friuli-Venezia Giulia) Fried *polenta* with beans and sauerkraut.

### Bistecca
Steak, usually of beef or veal. *B. alla fiorentina*: T-bone steak, properly from Val de Chiana beef, grilled over an open fire; also known as just *fiorentina. Bistecche alla valusina*: sautéed veal slices with cheese sauce. *B. di cavallo al uso selvatico* (Veneto): horse steaks simmered in wine and herbs, served with *polenta. B. all'amburghese*: hamburgers.

### Bistecchina
Thin steak.

### Bitto
(Lombardia) Cow's and goat's milk fat cheese, soft and buttery when young, sharper with age.

### Blanc de la Salle/de Morgex
(Valle d'Aosta) Dry white wines, rarely seen in commerce.

### Blauburgunder
See *Pinot.*

### (Al) Blu
Poached when just killed or alive, of freshwater fish.

## (Alla) Bobbiese
In the style of Bobbio, *Emilia-Romagna*. See *lumache*.

## Bobe
Type of sea bream.

## Boca
(Piemonte) Red *DOC* wine based on *Nebbiolo* grapes, of limited distribution.

## Bocca d'oro
Meagre, large sea fish with golden throat.
*Bocca negra*: dogfish.

## Bocconcini
Variety of meanings, from a light stew of diced meat, to thin slices of veal and ham rolled around cheese and cooked in butter. *B. fritti*: fried morsels, of cheese, sausage, bacon etc., as an appetizer or first course. *B. alla modenese*: bread sandwiched with ham and cheese, deep fried.

## Bocconotti
(Lazio) Sweet fritters or tarts, sometimes with *ricotta* cheese, candied fruits and spices.
*B. alla bolognese*: vol-au-vents filled with chicken livers, sweetbreads and truffle.

## Bodoletti
(Veneto) Top-shells, type of shellfish, often baked in the shells with oil and bayleaves.

## (Alla) Boema
Bohemian-style. See *lepre*.

## Boghe
Bogue, type of sea bream, common in *Liguria*.

## Bogoni
(Veneto) Snails.

## Boldro
(Toscana, Liguria) Monkfish.

## Bolgheri
(Toscana) Home of the famous *Sassicaia* wine; also a new *DOC* for dry white wine based on *Trebbiano* grapes.

## Bolla
World-famous producers of *Veneto* wines.

## Bollito
Boiled. Boiled beef. *Bollito misto* (Piemonte, Lombardia, Emilia-Romagna): mixed boiled meats, which may include beef, tongue, veal, calf's head, chicken, turkey, sausage; the mark of a good restaurant, served from a special trolley with the meats carved at table and presented with a piquant sauce and perhaps grated horseradish, boiled potatoes.

## (Alla) Bolognese
In the style of Bologna, *Emilia-Romagna*. Of pasta and sometimes other dishes, served with the characteristic meat sauce (*ragù*). Of veal escalopes, chicken or turkey breasts, breaded and fried, with ham and cheese, and perhaps white truffles. See also *baccalà, bocconotti, crescentina, fegatelli, lasagna, stecchi, tortellini, trippa*.

**(Alla) Bolzanese**
In the style of Bolzano, *Trentino-Alto Adige*. See *polenta, zuppa*.

**Bomba di riso**
(Emilia-Romagna) Baked rice mould with pigeons.

**Bombino**
(Puglia) Grape variety, both red and white.

**Bombolette**
Fritters.

**Bombolini**
(Veneto) Small deep fried dumplings.

**Bonarda**
(Lombardia, Piemonte, Emilia-Romagna) Red grape variety.

**Bond(i)ola**
(Veneto) Pork or veal and red wine sausage, smoked or dried.

**Bonet**
(Piemonte) Rum-flavoured custard cream with crushed macaroons.

**Bonita**
Small tuna fish.

**Boreto**
See *brodetto*.

**(Alla) Borghese**
'Bourgeois-style'. See *fegato, lingua, oca, patate, piselli, quaglie, trippa*.

**(Alla) Borgia**
In the style of the Borgias. See *caffè*.

**(Alla) Borgomanerese**
In the style of Borgomanero, *Piemonte*. See *tapulòn*.

**Borlotti**
See *fagioli*.

**Borraggine**
Borage, the herb.

**Bosa**
(Sardegna) Small port and its *DOC* dessert or aperitif wine from *Malvasia*.

**(Alla) Boscaiola**
'Forester's style'. With mushrooms.

**Bosco**
Wood. *Di bosco/dei boschi*: wild, e.g. of mushrooms.

**Bosega**
Grey mullet.

## Bosine
(Lombardia) Miniscule lake fish, often baked with cheese and spices as a flat cake.

## Bostrengo
(Marche) Rice cake with chocolate and pine nuts.

## Botarga
See *bottarga*.

## Botolo
Grey mullet.

## Bottagio
(Lombardia) Stew of pork ribs, rinds, ham, sausage, pig's trotters and cabbage; also known as *cazzoeula, posciandra*.

## Bottarga
(Sardegna, Sicilia, Calabria, Puglia, Liguria, Veneto) Pressed dried salted roe of tuna or mullet, often packed into a sausage shape; also known as *botarga, butarega, buttariga, ovotàrica*.

## Bottatrice
Freshwater fish.

## Botticino
(Lombardia) Small town known locally for dry red *DOC* wine.

## Bottigliera
Wine shop.

## Boudin
(Valle d'Aosta) Blood pudding.

## Bovol(on)i/bovoletti
(Veneto) Snails.

*Bovolo*: snail-shaped bread roll.

## Bozner Leiten
See *Colli Bolzano*.

## Bra
(Piemonte) Lightly salted white cheese.

## (Alla) Brace/bracia
On embers, charcoal grilled.

## Brachetto
(Piemonte) Red grape variety, making sweet, usually sparkling wines.

## Braciole
Steaks, slices of beef, veal, lamb, or fish, often skewered and grilled over coals. Chops, of pork. See also *braciolone*.

## Braciolette
Several meanings, from stuffed veal rolls, to lamb cutlets or slices. *B. di carne macinata* (Campania): minced meat patties baked on skewers with bread slices. *B. di melanzane ripiene*: grilled aubergine and bacon cubes on skewers.

## Bracioline
Small cutlets, steaks, of lamb.

## Braciolone
Large slice of beef or veal rolled round a stuffing and braised; different versions throughout Italy, and known as *braciole* in the south. *B. alla napoletana*: beef stuffed with ham, hard-boiled eggs, cheese, simmered with tomatoes. *B. all' urbinate*: stuffed with ham and sausage, braised in white wine.

## Bramaterra
(Piemonte) Village producing fine red *DOC* wine based on *Nebbiolo* grapes.

## Brand de cujun
See *stoccafisso*.

## Branzino
(Adriatic coast) Sea bass. *B. alla rivierasca*: baked with artichokes.

## Brasadee
(Lombardia) Ring-shaped cakes.

## Brasato
Braised. (Piemonte, Lombardia) Large piece of meat, usually beef, often marinated in red wine, then browned in fat and cooked slowly with liquid and aromatics.

## Brasciole
(Puglia) Veal rolls stuffed with ham and cheese, simmered in tomato sauce and served with pasta.

## Breganze
(Veneto) *DOC* zone producing red and white wines, mostly named according to grape variety.

## Bresaola
(Lombardia) Cured dried beef fillet, served in thin slices as a first course.

## Brigidini
(Toscana) Aniseed cakes.

## (Alla) Brindisana
In the style of Brindisi, *Puglia*. See *cicoria*.

## Brindisi
(Puglia) Port and *DOC* zone producing red and rosé wines based on *Negroamaro* grapes.

## Briosca
Brioche.

## Brisago
Cheese made from whey.

## Broada/broade
(Friuli) Turnips pickled with grape pressings, usually sliced and fried with onions and parsley, to accompany pork, turkey or soup; also known as *brovada*.

## Broccoli
Broccoli; or sometimes, confusingly, cauliflower (*cavolfiore*). *B. alla romana*: braised with white wine, oil and garlic. *B. alla siciliana*: stewed with oil, wine, olives, anchovies and cheese. *B. all' umbra*: simmered with anchovies, onions, white wine.

*Broccoli/broccoletti di rape/rapa*: turnip tops; also known as *cime di rape*. Broccoli-rave, with long slender stalks and tiny florets; also known as *broccoli di foglia, friarelli*.

## Brochat
(Valle d'Aosta) Thick wine custard eaten with rye bread.

## (A) Brodettato
Finished with egg yolks and lemon, of light stews, particularly lamb.

## Brodetto
(Adriatic coast) Fish soup, with numerous local versions all claiming to be the best; also known as *boreto, broeto*. The most celebrated include *b. all'anconetana*: with at least 13 different fish; *b. alla gradese*: with garlic, oil and vinegar; *b. alla ravennate*: squid, eel, red mullet etc., tomatoes, herbs, with the liquid and fish served in separate dishes; *b. veneziano*: made with various bony fish to flavour the stock plus pieces of superior fish – grey mullet, monkfish, octopus – kept whole, and served with slices of fried bread.

*Brodetto (pasquale) alla romana*: based on beef and lamb, finished with egg yolks and parmesan, traditional at Easter. See also *licurdia*.

## Brodo
Broth, clear consommé or bouillon, served as soup. *B. ristretto*: strong, concentrated, consommé. *B. pieno* (Calabria): with breadcrumbs, eggs and cheese.

*Brodo di giuggiolè* (Lombardia): sweet syrup of jujube fruits, quince, raisins, red wine, served in pastry with cream cheese.

## Broeto
See *brodetto*.

## Brofadei
(Lombardia) Meat broth with small fried pastry squares.

## Brolio
Probably the most famous *Chianti* estate, owned by Baron Ricasoli whose ancestors created modern Chianti.

## Bros(s)
(Piemonte) Cheese fermented with *grappa* or vinegar.

## Brovada
See *broada*.

## Brunello
See *Montalcino*.

## Bruscàndoli
(Veneto) Hop shoots, often cooked with rice.

## Bruschetta
(Lazio) Garlic toast soaked in olive oil.

## Bruscitt
(Lombardia) Beef paste with fennel seeds and wine, served with *polenta*.

**Brusco**
Sharp, sour.

**Brustengolo**
(Umbria) *Polenta* pie with apples and nuts.

**Brut**
Dry, of sparkling wine.

**Buca**
(Toscana) Small eating place, often without a written menu.

**(Alla) Bucaniera**
'Pirate-style'. With seafood and tomato sauce, of pasta.

**Bucatini**
Long hollow pasta noodles.

**Buccellato**
(Toscana) Sweet ring-shaped cake.

**Buccuno**
(Sicilia, Sardegna) Murex, small shellfish.

**Budellacci**
(Umbria) Smoked pig's offal with fennel seeds and garlic, usually grilled.

**Budelline**
Innards.

**Budello**
Intestine, gut.

**Budino**
Pudding, e.g. of rice. Savoury dumpling, quenelle, mousse, e.g. of chicken. *B. toscano*: baked sweetened *ricotta* cheese with ground almonds, raisins, eggs.

**Bue**
Beef, technically from an older animal. Ox, bullock.

**Buf(f)ala/bufalo**
Buffalo, whose milk is used for genuine *mozzarella* and other cheeses, but is increasingly rare.

**Bufalina**
See *mozzarella*.

**Bugì**
(Piemonte) Boiled beef.

**Buiabesa**
(Liguria) Fish soup, Genoese equivalent of the French 'bouillabaisse'.

**Büiì**
(Piemonte) Mixed boiled meats (*bollito misto*).

## Buricchi
(Emilia-Romagna) Almond pastry puffs.

## Burida
(Liguria) Stew of dried cod with tomatoes, mushrooms, anchovies; also known as *stoccafisso in tocchetti.*

## Burlenghi
(Emilia-Romagna) Pastry fritters with bacon, herbs and cheese.

## Burrata
(Puglia) Cheese made up of *caciocavallo* enclosing *mozzarella.*

## Burri(no)
(Molise, Calabria) Mild cheese enclosing a lump of butter; also known as *buttiri, manteche.*

## Burrida
(Sardegna) Fish stew with vinegar and nuts, served cold.

## Burro
Butter. *B. nero/nocciola*: butter heated to a dark/light brown with lemon or vinegar and capers, for fish.

## Burtleìna
(Emilia-Romagna) Small fried pastry squares, sometimes stuffed with ham.

## Busecca
(Lombardia) Rich tripe and bean soup.

## Busecchin
(Lombardia) Blood pudding with cream, cheese and spices, boiled.

**Busecchina**
(Lombardia) Boiled chestnuts with wine and cream.

**Bus(s)ola(no)**
(Lombardia, Veneto) Spicy nut and chocolate cake.

**Butarega**
See *bottarga*.

**Buttafuoco**
(Lombardia) 'Fire-thrower'. Excellent red *DOC* wine based on *Barbera* grapes.

**Buttariga**
See *bottarga*.

**Buttiri**
See *burrino*.

**Buzolai**
(Friuli-Venezia Giulia) Biscuits.

## Cabernet
Red grape variety, native of Bordeaux, grown in the north both as Cabernet franc and Cabernet sauvignon.

## Cacc'e Mmitte
(Puglia) 'Quaff and fill up'. Dry red *DOC* wine.

## Cacciagione
Game.

## (Alla) Cacciatora
'Hunter's style'. With a sauce based on tomatoes, onions, mushrooms, herbs and wine. See also *abbacchio, cinghiale, pollo*.
*Cacciatoro*: small version of type of sausage (*salame milano*).

## Cacciucco (Livornese)
Fish stew with many different versions, but essentially of cheap fish like rascasse, gurnard and conger eel, plus small cuttlefish or octopus, and often shellfish, cooked with hot red peppers, tomatoes and herbs; served with the fish pieces on garlic toast, moistened with the cooking juices.

## Cacio/caciu
Cheese. *C. all' argintera*: fried cheese with garlic, oregano and vinegar. *C. forte* (Campania): strong cheese, served as an appetizer.

## Caciocavallo
(Campania, Sicilia) Smooth mild smoky cheese becoming sharper and drier with age, of cow's milk sometimes with sheep or goat's milk added; the name ('cheese on horseback') may derive from the fact that it is strung together in pairs, or was originally made from mare's milk, or was stamped with a horse, the seal of Naples.

## Cacioricotta
(Abruzzo) Sheep's milk curds flavoured with coffee and lemon.

## Caciotta/caciotto
(central and S Italy) Semi-hard cheese of sheep's, cow's or goat's milk.

## Caciun(itt)i
(Marche) Small chocolate pastries.

## Cacuòcciuoli
See *risotto*.

## (Alla) Cadorina
See *gnocchi*.

## Caffè
Coffee. *C. alla Borgia* (Veneto): laced with apricot brandy, sprinkled with cinnamon. *C. cappucino*: with hot whipped milk, sprinkled with chocolate. *C. corretto* (Lombardia): laced ('corrected') with *grappa*. *C. espresso*: strong black coffee in a small cup. *C. latte*: with hot milk in equal parts, for breakfast. *C. valdostano*: laced with *grappa*, plus lemon peel, and passed round after a meal in a special pot with spouts, erroneously called *grolla*.

## Caggiunitti
(Abruzzo) Small sweet fritters.

## Cagliari
(Sardegna) Capital and *DOC* zone producing a wide range of aperitif, dessert and table wines named according to grape variety.

## (Alla) Cagliaritana
In the style of Cagliari, *Sardegna*. See *pizza*.

## (In) Cagnone
See *riso*.

## Caicc
(Lombardia) Large pasta squares filled with meat and cheese, served with butter and cheese.

## (Alla) Calabrese
In the style of *Calabria*. See *capretto, peperoni, ravioli, sgombro, soffritto, tonno*.

## Calamar(ett)i/calamaroni
Squid; or sometimes, confusingly, cuttlefish (*seppie*). *C. alla barese*: fried, with tomato and garlic sauce.

## Calascioni
(Lazio) Large baked pasta packets stuffed with *ricotta* cheese or vegetables.

## Calcionetti (alla chietina)
Apple and almond fritters.

## Calcioni
(Marche) Pasta squares stuffed with cheese, eggs, lemon and sugar; also known as *ravioli all' ascolana*.

(Molise) Fried pizza-type rounds with ham and cheese.

## Caldariello
(Puglia) Lamb stew with sheep's milk and fennel, served on slices of bread.

## Caldaro
(Alto Adige) Small lake and *DOC* for light fresh red wine, made mainly from *Schiava* grapes and produced in large quantities, often for export; also known as *Lago di Caldaro* and *Kalterersee*.

## Caldibona
(Marche) Savoury crescent-shaped fritters.

## Caldo
Hot.

## (Alla) California
See *manzo*.

## Caluso

(Piemonte) Small town noted for *DOC* wines made from *Erbaluce* grapes.

## Calzagatti

(Emilia-Romagna) Mixed *polenta* and beans, with ham and tomatoes.

## Calzoncini

(Basilicata) Half-moons of pasta filled with cheese, sugar, spices, served with meat sauce.

## Calzone

(Campania, Puglia, Basilicata) Baked round of yeast dough similar to large pizza, filled with ham and cheese in the classic Neapolitan version, or with onions, olives, anchovies, capers and cheese. *Calzoni* (Puglia): smaller rounds, either baked or fried, with various toppings; also known as *calzengiide, calzuncieddi, panzerotti.*

## (In) Camicia

'In a shirt'. Poached, of eggs. Baked in their jackets, of potatoes. See also *alosa.*

## Camoscio

Chamois. *C. alla tirolese*: marinated, then stewed with red wine and sour cream. *C. alla valdostana*: similar with *grappa* instead of cream, served with *polenta.*

## (Di) Campagna/(alla) campagn(u)ola

'Country-style'. See *risotto, uccelletti.*

## (Alla) Campanaro

(Veneto) 'Bellringer's style'. See *coniglio.*

## Campari
World-famous aperitif bitters, pink, alcohol-based, made by Fratelli Campari of Milan, *Lombardia*. *C.-soda*: bottled single portion aperitif.

## Campidano di Terralba
(Sicilia) Dry red *DOC* wine.

## Campo
Field. *Di campo*: wild, e.g. of asparagus.

## Canaiolo
Red grape variety used in *Chianti* and elsewhere.

## (Alla) Canavesana
In the style of Pont Canavese, *Piemonte*. See *coniglio*, *riso*, *tofeja*, *zuppa*.

## Candito
Candied, crystallized.

## Canederli
(Trentino-Alto Adige) Bread, bacon and sausage dumplings; also known as *caniderli*.

## Canesca
Shark.

## Canestrato
See *pecorino*.

## Canestrelli
Small scallops.
(Liguria, Piemonte) Sweet pastries.

## (Alla) Canevera
See *cappone*.

## Caniderli
See *canederli*.

## Caniscione
(Campania) Large type of pizza with rich cheese, ham and sausage filling, or anchovy and greens.

## Cannariculi
(Calabria) Thick fritters with honey or sugar.

## Cannaruòzzoli
(Calabria) Small pasta tubes, served with cheese and a sauce.

## Cannella
Cinnamon, the spice.

## Cannellini
See *fagioli*.

## Cannelloni
(Piemonte) Oblongs of pasta rolled up, typically with a meat stuffing and béchamel sauce, and browned in the oven. *C. alla Barbaroux*: filled with veal, ham and cheese, named after a royal official. *C. alla maniera di Limone*: stuffed with beef, ham and spinach. *C. alla partenopea*: filled with cheese and ham, with tomato and basil sauce.

## Cannochie
Mantis shrimps. *C. all'abruzzese*: cooked in wine, served with oil, lemon and hot pepper.

## Cannoli
(Sicilia) Pastry cylinders filled with sweetened *ricotta* cheese, nuts, candied fruit.

## Cannolicchi
Razor-shells.
*Cannoli(o)cchi/cannolicchieti*: small pasta tubes.

## Cannonau
(Sardegna) Grape variety, making strong red wines, both dry and sweet.

## Canosa
(Puglia) Dry red *DOC* wine.

## Cantina
Cellar. *C. sociale*: wine cooperative.

## Cantucci
(Toscana) Aniseed or almond biscuits.

## Cantunzein
See *pappardelle*.

**(Alla) Canzanese**
In the style of Canzano, *Abruzzo*. See *tacchino*.

**Cape**
(Veneto) Various shellfish. C. *longhe*: razor-shells. C. *sante*: scallops.

**Caparon/caparozzolo**
(Veneto) Sea truffle, shellfish.

**Capelli d'angelo/capellini**
Very narrow thin noodles, used in soups.

**Capena**
(Lazio) Dry white wine *(DOC)*.

**Caperzzoli**
Molluscs.

**Capiddi d'angilu**
(Calabria) Very thin noodles.

**Capillari**
Tiny eels.

**Capitone**
Large eel.

**Capocollo**
(Umbria, Puglia, Calabria) Dried lightly smoked pork sausage; also known as *coppa*.

**Caponata (palermitana)**
Dome-shaped salad of fried aubergines, celery and other vegetables, with olives, capers, anchovies, tomato sauce.
(Liguria) *Caponata (alla marinara)*: stale bread or biscuits soaked in oil and mixed with garlic, olives, anchovies etc.

**Capone**
(Sicilia) Dolphin fish. C. *apparecchiato*: fried slices with vinegar, caper, olives, served cold.

**Caponet**
(Piemonte) Fried courgette flowers, stuffed with veal, sausage and herbs.

**Cappe**
Bivalve molluscs. C. *liscia*: smooth Venus, small shellfish.

**Cappelle (di fungo)**
Mushroom caps.

**Cappellaci**
(Emilia-Romagna) Little pasta parcels with a stuffing, usually of pumpkin.

**Cappellano**
See *merluzzo*.

## Cappelletti

(Romagna, Umbria, Marche) Small peaked 'hats' of pasta stuffed with chicken, pork, sausage, cheese and spices; traditionally served in capon broth at Christmas.

## Cappello

'Hat'. *C. da gendarme* (Puglia, Basilicata): large cold pie filled with meat, hard-boiled eggs, cheese, macaroni, aubergines etc., in conical shape like a policeman's helmet; also known as *pasticcio d'inverno alla barese*.
*C. da prete* (Emilia-Romagna): salt dried pig's leg with spices, in tricorn shape like a priest's hat, boiled and served with a herb sauce.

## Cappelloni

(Lombardia) Large pasta envelopes stuffed with beef and sausage.

## Capperi

Capers.

## Cappieddi 'i prievidi

(Calabria) Small tricorn pasta shapes, served with cheese and a sauce.

## Capponada/capponata

(Liguria, Sardegna) Simpler version of *cappon magro*, based on tomatoes and tuna; also known as *cappunadda*.

## Cappone

Capon, castrated chicken. *C. alla canevera* (Veneto): boiled in an ox bladder, with a straw ('canevera' in dialect) as a vent.

Gurnard, sea fish. See also *pesce*.

*Capponi*: small red mullet.

## Cappon magro
(Liguria) Elaborate salad of mixed vegetables, fine fish and crustaceans, piled into a pyramid on a base of ship's biscuit and covered with a rich garlic and anchovy sauce.

## (Alla) Cappuccina
'Capuchin monk's style'. See *baccalà, carpa, minestra.*

## Cappuccino
Nasturtium leaves. See also *caffè.*

## (A) Cappuccio
See *lattuga.*

## Cappunadda
See *capponada.*

## Capra
Goat.
*Capra di mare*: spider crab.

## (Alla) Caprese
In the style of the isle of Capri, *Campania*. See *ravioli.*

## Capretto
Kid, young goat. *C. all'ascolana*: roast with herbs and marsala. *C. all' avellinese*: baked with parmesan and potatoes. *C. ripieno alla calabrese*: stuffed with the offal, tomatoes, hot pepper etc. and roast. *C. r. alla limonese*: stuffed with spinach, brains and cheese, roast. *C. alla piacentina*: stewed in white wine. *C. a sciusciareddu* (Sicilia): stewed with tomatoes, artichokes, asparagus.

## Capri
Island, with *DOC* for red and white wines, often grown on the mainland as well and very popular locally.

**Capriano del Colle**
(Lombardia) Red and white *DOC* wines from the town of that name.

**Capriccioso**
See *insalata*.

**(Alla) Caprilese**
In the style of Caprile, *Veneto*. See *capriolo*.

**Capri(u)olo/capriola**
Roebuck, roe deer, venison. *C. alla caprilese*: haunch stewed with bacon, calf liver, sage and white wine.

**Capuni**
(Sicilia) Dolphin fish.

**(Alla) Carabiniera**
'Carabiniere-style' See *acciughe*.

**Caragnoli**
(Molise) Honey pancakes.

**Caragoli**
(Veneto) Top-shells; or horn-shells.

**Caramei**
(Veneto) Fan-shaped confection of caramelized nuts, figs, apricots; also known as *golosessi*.

**Caramell(izz)ato**
Caramelized, candied, glazed.

**Carboj**
(Sicilia) Trade name for wines made by cooperative at Sciacca.

**(Alla) Carbonara**
'Charcoal-burner's style'. (Lazio) With bacon and eggs, of pasta, particularly spaghetti.
In the style of Carbonara, *Puglia*. See *agnello*.

**Carbonade/carbonata**
(Piemonte, Valle d'Aosta) Beef, or salt beef, and red wine stew, often served with *polenta*.

**Carciofi**
Globe artichokes. *C. ripiene di Agrigento*: stuffed with sardines, sausage and cheese, baked. *C. all'inferno*: baked with garlic, capers and pepper. *C. alla giudia* (Lazio): crisp fried. *C. alla matticella* (Lazio): baked over an open fire ('matticellà') with oil, garlic, mint. *C. alla romana*: braised with oil and herbs. *C. alla veneziana*: braised small ones. *C. al verde* (Sardegna): stewed in oil with herbs, plus beaten eggs. *C. alla villana palermitana* deep fried.
*Carciofini*: small artichokes, artichoke hearts.
*Carciofi di Giudea*: Jerusalem artichokes.

## Cardi

Cardoons. *C. al grifo* (Umbria): egg-and-breadcrumbed and fried, with veal slices, chicken livers and tomato sauce. *C. alla milanese*: baked with butter and parmesan. *C. alla perugina*: battered and fried. *C. alla sarda*: boiled, sprinkled with hard-boiled egg, parsley and breadcrumbs.

## (Alla) Cardinale

'Cardinal's style'. See *arancio*.

## Cardon(cell)i

Cardoons.

## Carema

(Piemonte) Small town known for distinguished red *DOC* wine from *Nebbiolo* grapes.

## Carignano

(Sardegna) Red grape variety, native of France.

## (Alla) Carlofortina

In the style of Carloforte, *Sardegna*. See *spaghetti*.

## Carmignano

(Toscano) Fine red *DOC* wine; originally sold as *Chianti*.

## Carne

Meat. *Carne cruda* (Piemonte): strips of raw veal or beef marinated in oil and lemon, served as a salad, sometimes with mushrooms and truffles added.

*Carne 'ncartarata* (Calabria): pressed boiled pork with hot pepper, served in slices with vegetable soup.

*Carnesecca*: (Toscana) bacon.

## Carnavala/carnevola

Carnival, Shrovetide.

## (Alla) Carniola

In the style of Carnia, *Friuli-Venezia Giulia*. See *testina*.

## Carot(in)e

Carrots.

## Carpa

Carp. *C. alla cappucina*: baked with herbs and lemon.

## Carpaccio

(Veneto) Very thinly sliced raw beef in a pale spicy sauce; invented by the famous restauranteur, Cipriani, and named after the Venetian painter known for his use of brilliant reds and whites.

## Carpano

Important company in Turin, *Piemonte*, said to have invented vermouth and known particularly for *Punt e Mes*.

## Carpeselle

(Abruzzo, Molise) Soused, of fish, the same method as *carpione*. *C. alla vastese*: garnished with pickled fruit and vegetables.

## Carp(i)o

Carp.

## (In) Carpione/carpionato

(Lombardia) Soused, of fish – fried, then marinated in oil with vinegar, white wine, herbs, spices and served cold.

## (A) Carrargiu

(Sardegna) Cooked 'in a hole' in the ground with a fire on top, of lamb, goat.

## Carrello

Trolley, of hors d'oeuvres, desserts.

## (Alla) Carrett(h)iera/carrattiera

'Cart driver's style'. (Lazio) With tuna and mushrooms, of pasta. See also *spaghettini*.

## (In) Carrozza

See *mozzarella*.

## (Alla) Carsolina

In the style of the Carso plateau of Trieste, *Friuli-Venezia Giulia*. See *minestra*.

## Carta di musica

See *pane*.

## Carteddate

(Puglia) Ribbon fritters soaked in honey or wine.

## Cartizze

See *Conegliano – Valdobriadene*.

**(In) Cartoccio**
Wrapped in paper cases or foil and baked, e.g. of fish, veal escalopes.

**(Di) Casa**
Homemade, of the house.
*Casa vinicola*: winery.

**(Alla) Casalinga**
'Housewife's style'. Homemade; simple, plain. See also *pizzella*.

**Casarecal**
(Marche) Sweet bun.

**Casatiello dolce**
(Campania) Sweet pastry; also known as *pigna di Pasqua*.

**Casca'**
(Sardegna) Couscous, steamed semolina, with vegetables and meat.

**(Alla maniera di) Cascia**
In the style of Cascia, *Umbria*. With anchovies, tomatoes, truffles, of pasta. See also *anguilla, frittata, strascinati*.

**Cascina**
Farmhouse.

**Casereccio**
Homemade, homely.
(Lazio, Puglia) Large bread loaf; also known as *barile*.

**(Alla) Casertana**
In the style of Caserta, *Campania*. See *zite*.

**Casigiola**
(Sardinia) Type of cheese.

## Caso forte
(Campania) Strong cheese made by traditional methods; also known as *saticulano*.

## Casoncelli/casonsei
(Lombardia) Sleeve-shaped pasta stuffed with sausage, spinach, raisins, cheese, or with beef, cheese and herbs, served with melted butter.

## Cassata (alla siciliana)
Authentically, rich sponge cake soaked in liqueur, layered with *ricotta* cheese and decorated with candied fruits and nuts; often with the addition of ice cream and chocolate in restaurants.

*Cassata abruzzese*: sweet nougat cake.

## Casseruola
Saucepan, casserole.

## Cassettine (siciliane)
Sweet almond pastries.

## Cassoeula/cassöla
(Lombardia, Piemonte) Pork and cabbage stew with white wine and sometimes goose, often served with *polenta*; many local versions.

## Cassola
(Sardegna) Fish soup with hot pepper and tomatoes, served with garlic toast.

## Cassoni
See *consum*.

## Castagnaccio
(Toscana, Liguria) Chestnut flour cake with pine nuts and herbs and perhaps raisins; also known as *pizza alla toscana*.

## Castagne
Chestnuts. *C. alla romagnola*: simmered in red wine.

## Castagnedde
(Puglia) Small almond pastries.

## Castagnole/castagnone
(Emilia-Romagna, Marche, Friuli) Sweet fritters.

Small sea fish, used in soups.

## Castel del Monte
(Puglia) Important *DOC* zone for red and rosé wines.

## (Di) Castelfranco
Of Castelfranco, *Veneto*. See *radicchio*.

## (Alla) Castellana
'Castle-style'. See *lumache*.

*Castellana di peperoni* (Piemonte): sweet peppers baked with ham and cheese.

**Casteller**
(Trentino-Alto Adige) Blended dry red *DOC* wine, mainly local distribution.

**Castelli di Jesi**
(Marche) *DOC* zone producing well known white wine from *Verdicchio* grapes.

**Castello**
Castle.

**Castelnuovo Don Bosco**
(Piemonte) Sweet red and sometimes sparkling wine *(DOC)*, from *Malvasia* grapes.

**Castlemagno**
(Piemonte) Herby *gorgonzola*-type cheese.

**Castradina**
(Veneto) Smoked and dried mutton, usually boiled with rice.

**Castrato**
Mutton. *Castratello*: lamb.

**Casunziei**
(Veneto) Pasta squares stuffed with pumpkin, spinach or chard, ham or cheese.

**(Alla) Catanese**
In the style of Catania, *Sicilia*. See *lasagnette, melanzane, pizza, sarde, spaghetti*.

**Catalogna**
See *cicoria*.

**(Alla) Catanzarese**
In the style of Catanzaro, *Calabria*. See *costolette, mursiellu*.

**Cauciuni**
(Puglia) Sweet fried pastries, filled with chick peas, chocolate, cinnamon.

**Cavallo**
Horse.
*Cavalla* (Liguria): mackerel.

**Cavallucci**
(Lazio) Small honey cakes in the form of a horse.

**Cavatelli**
(Puglia, Calabria, Basilicata, Molise) Hard shell-shaped pasta, moulded by hand, often cooked with greens and herbs, dressed with oil, garlic and hot pepper or with cheese; also known as *rascatelli, richiele, ricchie 'i prieviti*.

**Cavatieddi**
See *mignuic*.

## Cavedano
Freshwater fish.

## Caviale
Caviar.

## Caviglione
Small gurnard, used in fish soups.

## Cavolata
(Sardegna) Cabbage, potato and pork soup.

## Cavolfiore
Cauliflower; sometimes also known as *broccoli. C. alla piemontese*: florets with onion, anchovy and marjoram. *C. a vastedda* (Sicilia): dipped in anchovy-flavoured butter and deep fried.

## Cavolini di Brusselle/Bruxelle
Brussel sprouts.

## Cavolo
Cabbage; or sometimes cauliflower. *C. acidi* (Friuli-Venezia Giulia): cooked in vinegar, garlic, herbs and fermented. *C. stufato alla veneziana*: shredded, stewed with oil, vinegar and garlic.

*C. broccoluto*: broccoli.

*C. nero*: black cabbage, kale- and broccoli-like vegetable. *C. n. alla tedesca*: stewed with vinegar, onion and caraway.

*C. rapa*: kohlrabi.

*C. rosso*: red cabbage. *C. r. di Agrigento*: stewed in oil, with vinegar, capers, olives; also known as *trunza di fera*.

## Cavreti de Gambellara
(Veneto) Goat kid's offal stuffed with herbs and spit-roasted.

## (In) Cavroman
See *ris*.

## Cazmarr
(Basilicata, Puglia) Lamb's offal baked or charcoal grilled; also known as *migliulatiello*.

## Cazzoeula/cazzuola di montone
(Lombardia) Mutton stew with ham, sausage, tomatoes and beans. See also *bottagio*.

## Cecchi
Important company for *Chianti* and *Orvieto* wines.

## Cecenielli/cecinielli
Tiny anchovies and sardines, deep fried.

## Ceci
Chick peas. *C. con la tempia* (Lombardia): soup with slices of pig's head.

## Cedioli/cèe
Tiny eels. *C. alla pisana*: fried alive in oil with garlic and sage, plus parmesan.

## Cedro
Citron. Sweet liqueur mader from citrons.

## Cefal(ett)o
Grey mullet.

**Cellatica**
(Lombardia) Dry red wine *(DOC)*.

**Cenci**
(Toscana) Sweet fritters, twisted in knots or bows.

**(Sotto la) Cenere**
Roasted in the ashes, e.g. of truffles.

**Centerbe**
Mint-flavoured liqueur supposed to contain 100 herbs; also known as *Silvestro*.

**Cepole**
Thin pink sea fish, used in soups.

**Cerasella**
Popular cherry liqueur.

**Cerasuolo**
Dark or cherry-coloured rosé, of wines.

**Ceresolini**
See *tajarin*.

**Cerfoglio**
Chervil, herb.

**Cerignola**
(Puglia) Town noted for dry red *DOC* wine.
Large green olives.

**Cernia**
Grouper, Mediterranean fish; also known as *luxerna*.

**(Alla) Certos(in)a**
'Carthusian monk-style'. See *manzo, mele, risotto*.

**Cervella/cervello**
Brains, usually calf's; often fried. *C. alla partenopea*: baked in oil with olives and capers.

**Cervellata**
(Puglia, Calabria) Pork and veal sausage with fennel seeds or hot pepper.

**Cerveteri**
(Lazio) Red and white *DOC* wines.

**Cervo**
Deer, stag, venison.

**Cesanese**
(Lazio) Red grape variety.

**(Alla) Cetrarese**
In the style of Cetraro, *Calabria*. See *sarde*.

**Cetrioli**
Cucumbers. *C. alla comasca*: thinly sliced, with onion, oil and vinegar. *C. alla toscana*: simmered in butter and cream.

**Cevapcici**
(Friuli-Venezia Giulia) Small mixed meat sausages, grilled or fried.

**Chambave**
(Valle d'Aosta) Small town producing *C. rouge*: robust red wine, and *Passito di C.*: sweet white wine from the *Moscato* grape; both mainly local distribution.

**Chardonnay**
White grape variety, aristocratic native of Burgundy; also known as *Pinot Chardonnay*.

**Chenelline**
Tiny dumplings, for soup.

**Cheppia**
Shad, migratory fish.

**Chiacchiere (della nonna)**
(Lombardia) Sweet pastry fritters, twisted into bows.

**Chianti**
(Toscana) Largest Italian *DOC* area, divided into 7 zones, *Classico*, Colli Aretini, Colli Fiorentino, Colli Senesi, Colline Pisane, Montalbano and Rufina and producing the popular red wine, from a blend of red *Sangiovese* and *Canaiolo* with the addition of white *Trebbiano* and *Malvasia; vecchio* indicates two years ageing and *reserva* three years. Many producers belong to a consortium, *Classico*, with the symbol of the black cockerel, being the most common. The area becomes *DOCG* with the 1984 vintage.

**Chiaretto**
'Claret'. Medium-coloured rosé wine, the best being from Lake Garda, *Lombardia*.

**Chieri**
(Piemonte) Small town and its light red *DOC* wine from *Fresia* grapes.

**(Alla) Chietina**
In the style of Chieti, *Abruzzo*. See *calcionetti, coniglio*.

**Chifel**
(Trentino-Alto Adige) Curved bread roll.

**Chiffer(on)i**
Curved pasta tubes.

**China**
Quinine. *Chinato*: treated or flavoured with quinine.

**Chinulille**
(Calabria) Fritters stuffed with *ricotta* cheese.

## Chiocciole (di vigna)

Snails. *C. a picchipacchio* (Sicilia): in tomato and onion sauce. *C. alla pugliese*: simmered in oil, wine and herbs, with hot pepper and wild fennel. See also *monzittas*.

*Chiocciole marine*: top-shells, small shellfish.

*Chiocciole*: small pasta shells, for soup.

## Chiocciolini

Spiral-shaped buns.

## Chiodi di garofano

Cloves, the spice.

## (Alla) Chioggiotta

In the style of Chioggia, *Veneto*. See *risotto*.

## Chisöl

(Lombardia) Sweet lemon tart. See also *schissoeula*.

## (Alla) Chitarra

See *maccheroni*.

## Chizze

(Emilia) Fried squares of bread dough, stuffed with cheese or vegetables.

## Ciabuscoli

See *ciaùscoli*.

## Ciaccia

(Marche) Type of pizza with eggs.

## Ciacci montanari

(Emilia-Romagna) *Ricotta* cheese dumplings, served with ham and sausage.

**Cial(led)da**
(Puglia) Onion and tomato soup with bread soaked in it.

**Cialde**
Waffles.

**Cialdoni**
(Lazio) Biscuit curls; also known as *cialde arrotolate.*

**Cialzons**
(Friuli-Venezia Giulia, Trentino-Alto Adige) Pasta packets stuffed with meat, eggs, cheese and herbs or with spinach and sultanas; also known as *ciarscons, cjalsons.*

**Ciambell(on)e/ciambelon**
(Liguria, Umbria, Romagna, Marche, Lazio) Ring-shaped cakes or pastries, often with aniseed, nuts, candied fruit and grape must; also known as *panafracchi.*
(Toscana, Sardegna) Bread loaves.

**Ciambotta/ciammotta/cianfotta**
(Calabria, Basilicata, Campania) Stewed potatoes, tomatoes, aubergines and peppers, eaten hot or cold.

**Ciâr (in padiele)**
(Friuli) Beef braised with horseradish, herbs and spices. See also *pastissada.*

**Ciaramicola**
(Umbria) Sweet yeast cake.

**Ciarimboli**
(Marche) Dried and spiced pork innards, grilled.

**Ciarscons**
See *cialzons.*

**Ciaudedda**
(Basilicata) Artichokes, beans, potatoes stewed in oil.

**Cia(b)ùscoli/ciaùsculu**
(Marche) Soft lightly smoked pork sausage, spread on bread.

**Cibreo**
(Toscana) Chicken giblets, liver and cockscombs cooked with egg yolks and lemon.

**Cicala (di mare)**
Flat lobster.

**Cicc**
(Lombardia) Fried *polenta* and cheese cake, sometimes sweet.

**Ciccioli**
Pork scratchings, crackling.

## Cicerata
See *cicirata*.

## Cicerello
Sand eel.

## Ciceri e tri(a)
(Puglia) Chick pea and pasta soup.

## Cicherchiata
(Abruzzo, Marche) Honey fritters in a ring or heart shape. (Umbria) Honey and almond cake.

## Ciciones
(Sardegna) Savoury dumplings, with meat and/or tomato sauce and cheese; also known as *gnocchi alla sassarese, malloreddus, macarones caidos, vitellini*.

## Cicirata
(Calabria, Basilicata) Tiny honey fritters; also known as *cicerata*.

## Cicoria
Curly endive, chicory. See also *radicchio*.
*Cicoria asparagio/di Catalonia/Catalogna*: asparagus chicory. *C. alla brindisana*: with tomato and bacon sauce.
*C. spadona*: sword-leaved green chicory, Belgian endive.
*Cicoriella*: wild chicory.

## Cieche
(Toscana) Tiny eels.

## Ciliege
Cherries.

## Cima
(Liguria) Elaborate dish of cold breast of veal stuffed with offal, eggs, artichokes, peas and herbs.

## Cime di rape

Turnip tops.

## Cinghiale

Wild boar. *C. alla cacciatora*: leg larded with ham, stewed in wine with onions, carrots etc.

## Cinque Terra

(Liguria) Small *DOC* area making dry white wine. *C. T. sciacchetra*: fortified dessert wine requiring 1 year ageing, local distribution.

## Cinzano

Famous firm of vermouth makers based in Turin, *Piemomte*.

## Cioccolata/cioccolato

Chocolate. *Cioccolatine*: chocolates.

## (Alla) Ciociara

(Lazio) 'Peasant-style'. See *cuore, fettucine, maccheroni, polenta, spezzatino*.

## Cioncia

(Toscana) Calf's head stew with hot pepper, spices and olives.

## Ciope

(Trentino-Alto Adige) Round bread roll; also known as *spaccatina*.

## Cipolle

Onions. *C. farcite alla grossetana*: stuffed with meat and mushrooms, braised.

*Cipolette/cipolline*: small onions, spring onions.

## Cipiduzzi/cipuddazzi/cipudrizze

(Puglia, Calabria) Wild bitter onion-type bulb, similar to grape hyacinth; also known as *lampascioni, lampasciuoli.*

## Ciriole

Tiny eels. *C. alla fiumarola* (Lazio): simmered with garlic, capers, anchovies, white wine.

(Lazio) Crusty round bread rolls.

*Ciriole alla ternana*: thick pasta strips, served with oil and garlic or a sauce.

## Cirò

(Calabria) *DOC* wines, red, white and rosé.

## Cisra

(Piemonte) Chick pea soup.

## Citrioli

Cucumbers.

## Ciufulitti

(Lazio) Homemade pasta noodles.

## Ciuppi(n)

(Liguria) Stew of rock fish, served on slices of bread.

## Civraxiu

(Sardegna) Huge solid bread loaf.

## Cjalsons

See *cialzons.*

## Classico

Classic.

Original or central vineyards of a *DOC* zone and the wines grown there, e.g. *Soave Classico, Chianti Classico.*

## Claviari

Type of fungus.

## Coada

See *sopa.*

## Cocciole

Cockles, shellfish.

## Cocciu

Star-gazer, sea fish.

## Cocciuleddas de meli

(Sardegna) Nut, spice and honey cakes.

## Cocco

See *noce.*

**Coc(c)oi(s) (de gerda)**
(Sardegna) Flat bread with pork bits and cheese.

**Cocomero**
Water melon.

**Cocone**
(Piemonte) Caesar's mushrooms.

**Coda**
Tail, of ox, scampi etc. *Coda (di bue) alla vaccinara* (Rome): oxtail braised with wine and vegetables, sultanas, pine nuts and chocolate.
*Coda di rospo*: monkfish.

**Codeghì**
(Lombardia) Dried pork sausage.

**Cogna**
(Piemonte) Spicy preserve of raisins, apples, figs, nuts, served with boiled meats.

**Cogneintze**
Of Cogne, *Valle d'Aosta*. See *soupe*.

**Coiettas**
(Sardegna) Cabbage rolls stuffed with meat.

**Cola**
(Puglia) Cauliflower, often served with pasta.

**Colli Albani**
(Lazio) Large *DOC* zone producing white wines, mainly dry, sometimes semi-sweet and sparkling.

**Colli Altotiberini**
(Umbria) *DOC* area producing red and dry white wines.

**Colli Apuani**
(Toscana) *DOC* area and its little-known dry white wine.

**Colli Berici**
(Veneto) *DOC* zone known for 7 wines named by grape variety.

**Colli Bolognesi di San Pietro/Monte San Pietro/dei Castelli Medioevali**
(Emilia-Romagna) *DOC* areas producing red and white wines; 6 types authorized, usually named according to grape variety.

**Colli di Bolzano**
(Alto Adige) *DOC* area making light, dry red *DOC* wine; also known as *Bozner Leiten*.

**Colli del Trasimeno**
(Umbria) *DOC* region for red and white wines; includes an estate owned by Lamborghini, the car maker.

## Colli Euganei
(Veneto) *DOC* area making red and white table wines and a sweet, sometimes sparkling, wine from *Moscato*.

## Colli Lanuvini
(Lazio) *DOC* zone making dry and semi-sweet white wines, mainly from *Malvasia*.

## Colli Maceratesi
(Marche) *DOC* area producing dry white wine based on *Trebbiano* grapes.

## Colli Morenici Mantovani del Garda
(Veneto) *DOC* area for red, white and rosé wines of local interest.

## Colli Orientali del Friuli
Large *DOC* region with 12 wines authorized and named according to grape variety. A rare semi-sweet dessert wine, *Picolit*, has its only *DOC* here.

## Colli Perugini
(Umbria) *DOC* zone for red, white and rosé wines.

## Colli Pesaresi
(Marche) *DOC* area for dry red wine based on *Sangiovese* grapes.

## Colli Tortonese
(Piemonte) *DOC* area making red wine from *Barbera* grapes and white from *Cortese*.

## Colline Lucchesi

(Toscana) *DOC* for dry red wine based on *Sangiovese*, mostly for local consumption.

## Collio (Goriziano)

(Friuli) *DOC* region particularly noted for its fine white wines; 11 types authorized, 10 named according to grape variety, the 11th being simply *Collio*, blended light dry slightly sparkling wine.

## Collo

Neck, of lamb etc.

## Colo de castra

(Veneto) Boiled mutton with celery and onion, served with rice and peas.

## Colomb(acci)o/colomba

Wood pigeon, dove, often hung till high. *Colombi alla maniera d'Amelia*: charcoal grilled on skewers, with white wine and olive sauce and fried bread spread with the entrails. *C. in salmi alla perugina*: marinated, then stewed with herbs, mushrooms, red wine. *C. stufati alla ternana*: stewed with ham and white wine, served with lentils. *C. all'umbra*: stewed with herbs and white wine.

*Colomba (pasquale)* (Lombardia): yeast bun with almonds. (Emilia-Romagna) Rich cake with apples, pears, raisins.

## Colonna

See *Montecompatri*.

## Colzetti

(Liguria) Small figure-of-eight pasta shapes.

## (Alla) Comasca
In the style of Como, *Lombardia*. See *agoni, cetrioli*.

## Composto
Composed, compound. *(In) composta*: compote, of fruit.

## Concentrato
Concentrated, concentrate, e.g. of tomatoes.

## Conchiglie
Shells. Scallop shells, as a container for hot preparations.
(Sicilia) Small shell-shaped cakes stuffed with citron.
*Conchiglie(tte)*: small pasta shells.
*Conchiglie dei pellegrini/Saint-Jacques*: scallops.

## Condiggion
(Liguria) Mixed salad – tomatoes, peppers, gherkins etc. – on a slice of bread.

## Condito
Seasoned. Dressed, of salad.
*Condita* (Abruzzo): bacon soup with beaten eggs and cheese; also known as *connita*.

## Conegliano-Valdobriadene
(Veneto) *DOC* zone producing dry white wines from *Prosecco* grapes. *Superiore di Cartizze: Prosecco* wine grown in defined area around Valdobriadene.

## Conero
(Marche) *DOC* for robust dry red wine based on *Montepulciano* grapes.

## Confetti
Sweetmeats, confectionery. *Confettato*: candied.

## Confettura
Jam.

## Confortini
(Piemonte) Long thin biscuits.

## Congelato
Frozen.

## Coniglio
Rabbit. *C. arrostito alla campanaro*: larded with bacon, roast, with lemon and butter sauce. *C. alla canavesana*: stewed with potatoes and meat broth. *C. alla chietina*: stuffed with ham and herbs, roast. *C. alla moda d'Ischia*: stewed in oil, white wine, tomatoes and herbs. *C. alla parmigiana*: with white wine, herbs, peppers, vegetables. *C. farcito/ripiene alla pesarese*: stuffed with the liver, heart, cheese and roasted, or stewed with calf's foot and served cold in jelly.

## (In) Conserva
Preserve, jam, of fruit, vegetables. Tinned. *Conservato*: preserved.

## Consorzio
Consortium, e.g. of wine growers.

## Consum
(Emilia-Romagna) Semi-circular pastries stuffed with greens, cooked on a griddle; also known as *cassoni* when fried.

## (Alla) Contadina
'Country-style'. See *acciughe, fegato, frittata, mus, sarde, tonno.*

## Conto
Bill.

## Contorno
Vegetable dish. Garnish.

## Controfiletto (di bue)
Sirloin, of beef.

## Convento
Convent, monastery.

## Copate/copete
(Toscana, Puglia) Small sweet wafer cakes.

## Copertino
(Puglia) Red and rosé *DOC* wines based on *Negroamaro* grapes.

## Coperto
Cover charge. *(Sotto) coperta*: one ingredient covered with another, e.g. a slice of cheese.

## Coppa
(Lombardia, Emilia) Salted and dried pork sausage; also known as *capocollo*. (Lazio) Brawn of pig's head. (Veneto) Loaf of ham, tongue and *mortadella*. (Umbria, Marche) Spicy pork sausage, sometimes eaten boiled.

*Coppa al forno* (Emilia-Romagna): pork fillet with rosemary, simmered in white wine.

Coupe, fruit and ice cream sundae. *Coppa torino*: sponge cake soaked in rum with cream and glazed chestnuts.

## Coppiette
(Toscana, Lazio) Dried smoked boar, horse or beef.

## Cora
Major producers of *vermouth* and *Asti spumante*.

## Corallo
Roe, coral, of lobster.

## Corat(ell)a
Offal. *C. di agnello alla sarda*: lamb's offal threaded on skewers with ham slices, wrapped in pig's caul and fried. *C. di a. del teramano*: stuffed into an intestine, fried.

## Coregone
See *lavarello.*

## Cord(ul)a
(Sardegna) Goat's or lamb's offal grilled over charcoal, or stewed with peas and beans; also known as *sa corda.*

## Cori
(Lazio) Red and white *DOC* wines, of local interest.

## Coriandro
Coriander, the spice.

## Cornetti
Pastry horns, usually filled with cream.

## (Alla) Corona
In a ring shape.

## Coronata
(Liguria) Light dry white wine.

## Cortese
Grape variety grown in north, making light crisp white wines. See also *Gavi* and *Monferrato.*

## Corvo
Corb, sea fish.

(Sicilia) Trade name of Casa Vinicola Duca di Salaparuta, making a range of non-*DOC* wines of international reputation.

## Corzetti

(Liguria) Tiny figure-of-eight pasta shapes, served with pine nuts and herbs or a sauce.

## Coscetta/coscetto

Leg, of lamb, poultry.

## Coscia/cosci(ott)o

Haunch, of venison; leg, of lamb, goat. *Cosciotto di agnello all'aretina*: of lamb, marinated and roast. *C. di a. all'abruzzese*: braised in wine with herbs and tomatoes. *C. di a. alla norcina*: pot-roasted with ham and wine, served with potatoes. *C. di a. pasquale*: larded with ham, braised in wine.

## Costa(ta)

Rib. Steak, escalope. *C. di maiale*: pork chop. *C. di manzo*: rib roast or T-bone steak, of beef.

Stalk. *Coste di biete*: chard stalks. *C. di sedano*: celery sticks.

## Costardello

Skipper, saury, sea fish.

## Costarelle/costi(ci)ne

Chops, spareribs of pork. *C. di maiale alla trevigiana*: cooked with garlic, sage and white wine.

## Co(s)tolett(in)e

Chops, of pork, lamb. Cutlets, escalopes, of veal. 'Cutlets', breast fillets, of poultry. Steaks, of venison. Legs, of frogs. *Costolette di agnello a scottadito* (Lazio): grilled ('burn-your-fingers') lamb chops, blackened on outside, pink within. *C. di a. alla catanzarese*: fried, garnished with anchovies, capers, mushrooms and artichokes. *C. di maiale alla modenese*: braised pork chops with sage, white wine and possibly tomatoes. *C. di m. del Montefeltro*: covered in salt, then grilled. *C. di m. alla napoletana*: fried, finished with garlic, peppers, tomatoes, mushrooms. *C. di m. all'umbra*: flattened and fried, served with wine and pickled cucumber sauce. *C. di vitello alla siciliana*: veal slices marinated in vinegar, coated in egg, garlic, cheese, breadcrumbs and fried. *C. di v. all Umberto di Savoia*: fried, served on toast with cheese sauce and truffles; after a 19th-century king of Italy. *C. di v. alla valdostana*: breaded and fried, with cheese, ham and perhaps truffles.

## Cotechinata

(Basilicata) Rolls of pork rind enclosing bacon and herbs, cooked with tomatoes, as a sauce for pasta.

## Cotechino

(Emilia-Romagna, Veneto, Lombardia) Large fresh pork sausage, lightly salted and spiced, usually boiled and served hot. C. *in galera* (Emilia-Romagna): wrapped in beef and ham slices ('in a galley') and simmered in red wine.

## Cotiche

Rinds, of pork.

## Côtletta 'd crin a l'astesana

Breaded pork chops baked with anchovies and truffles.

## Cotogne

Quinces. *Cotognata/cotognato* (Sicilia): quince preserve, jam.

## Cotolette

See *costolette*.

## Cottene

Rinds, of pork.

## Cotto

Cooked, baked.

## Coturnice

Partridge. Quail.

## Cozze

Mussels, shellfish. C. *alla barese*: finished in the oven with cheese sauce. C. *alla leccese*: cooked with oil, lemon, parsley.

## Cozzula

(Sardegna) Type of bread.

## Crauti

(Trentino-Alto Adige) Sauerkraut.

## Crema

Custard, custard cream dessert. C. *fritta*: fried custard in diamond shapes, served with meat or as a dessert. C. *di mascherpone*: cream cheese mixed with sugar, egg yolks and liqueur. C. *pasticcera*: confectioner's custard.

Cream soup.

Sweet liqueur.

*Crema di latte*: cream.

## (Alla) Cremasca

In the style of Crema, *Lombardia*. See *tortelli*.

## (Di) Cremona

Of Cremona, *Lombardia*. See *mostarda*.

### Cren
(Friuli-Venezia Giulia) Horseradish.

### Crescentina (bolognese)
Flat bread studded with bacon.
*Crescentine* (Toscana): fried squares of bread dough, savoury or sweet.

### Crescenza
(Lombardia, Piemonte, Veneto) Soft square version of *stracchino* cheese, creamy and mild.

### Crescia
(Marche) Fritters or light pastries, either savoury or sweet.

### Crescioni
Watercress.
Deep-fried pasta triangles filled with spinach and cream.

### Crespelle/crespolini
Pancakes, often stuffed with spinach, ham, cheese etc., covered in béchamel and finished in the oven. *Crespelle 'mbusse alla maniera del teramano*: stuffed with beef, ham and chicken giblets, served with broth and cheese.

### Crespone
See *salame*.

### (Alla) Creta
Baked in clay, especially of pheasant.

### Crispeddi
(Sicilia) Type of fried pizzas filled with *ricotta* cheese or anchovies.

### Crispelle
(Sicilia, Molise) Small fried rounds of pizza dough, or sweet fritters.

### Croccante
Crisp, crunchy. Praline, almond brittle.
*Croccanti* (Toscana): almond biscuits.

### Crocchette
Croquettes, e.g. of spinach, brains, *polenta*, usually breadcrumbed and fried.

### Crocette
Small cone-shaped shellfish.
(Emilia-Romagna) Crisp bread rolls.

### Crosetti
(Emilia-Romagna) Homemade pasta discs, served with a sauce.

### Crostacei
Crustaceans.

## Crostat(in)a

Tart, often of fruit or jam. *C. dolce alla romana*: cherry custard pie.
Savoury pie. *Crostate alla perugina*: rounds of bread stuffed with chicken, quails, truffles.

## Crostato

With a crust, browned. See also *lepre*.

## Croste

Crusts. Filled tartlets made with hollowed bread slices, savoury or sweet.

## Crostini/crostoncini

Croutons, fried bread cubes, as a garnish for soup. Canapés, slices of fried bread or toast with a topping, as a first course. *C. napoletani*: covered with *mozzarella* cheese, anchovy and tomato, baked. *C. alla maniera dell'Umbria*: with truffles and anchovies.

## Crostoli

(Marche) Flat griddle cakes, served with ham or cheese.

## (Sul) Crostone

On toast.

**Crucetta**
(Calabria) Roast figs stuffed with nuts.

**Crudo**
Raw, uncooked.

**Crumiri**
(Piemonte) Sweet biscuits.

**Cruti**
(Trentino-Alto Adige) Sauerkraut.

**Cuata**
See *zuppa*.

**Cubbaita**
(Calabria, Sicilia) Honey, almond and sesame seed sweetmeat; also known as *cumpittu*.

**Cuccia**
(Sicilia) Wheat pudding.

**Cucina**
Kitchen. Cooking, cuisine.

**Cuculli di patate**
(Liguria) Potato fritters with cheese and pine nuts, or simply pancakes with potato cubes.

**Cuddiruni di Agrigento**
Pizza with tomato, cheese and sardine topping; also known as *pizza cuddiruni*.

**Culaccio**
Rump, of beef.

**Culatello**
(Emilia-Romagna) Rump of pork salted, spiced and matured for at least a year.

**Culingiones/culurjones**
(Sardegna) Squares of pasta or potato dough, stuffed with cheese, perhaps mint or saffron, served with a sauce; also known as *angiulottus*.

**Cumino**
Cumin, the spice.

**Cumpittu**
See *cubbaita*.

**(Alla) Cuneese**
In the style of Cuneo, *Piemonte*. See *fresse, gnocchi, lümasse*.
*Cuneesi al rum*: small meringues soaked in rum and dipped in chocolate.

**Cunsa/cunscia**
See *pasta, polenta*.

**Cuoccio**
Gurnard, sea fish.

**Cuoco**
Cook, chef.

**Cuore**
Heart, of ox, veal, of celery etc. *C. di vitello alla ciociara*: calf heart marinated in oil and herbs, stewed. *C. di v. ai ferri alla trentina*: marinated and grilled.
Cockle, shellfish.

**Cuoriccini**
(Sicilia) Heart-shaped biscuits, traditional at weddings.

**Curadura**
(Lombardia) Salted dried lake fish *(agoni)*, fried as a flat cake and eaten with *polenta*.

**Curritholata**
(Sardegna) Bean, sausage and fennel soup.

**Cuscinetto**
(Lazio) Small rectangular bread loaf.
*Cuscinetti*: hollowed bread slices with a filling.

**Cuscusu**
(Sicilia) Couscous, steamed semolina, usually served with seafood. *C. alla livornese*: with cabbage, meat balls and tomato sauce.

**Custoza**
(Veneto) Centre of sizeable *DOC* area for light dry blended white wines.

**Cutturidde/cutturieddu**
(Puglia, Basilicata) Lamb stew with tomatoes, onions, cheese and herbs.

**(A) Cutturo**
See *agnello*.

**Cynar**
Dark brown aperitif bitters based on artichokes.

## Dad(in)i
Small cubes, dice.

## Dame
Small raisin cakes.

## Datteri
Dates.

*Datteri di mare*: date-shells, similar to mussels. *D. di m. stufati alla ligure*: stewed with garlic, parsley, tomatoes.

## Delizie
Delights, delicacies.

## Denominazione di Origine Controllata (DOC)
Controlled name or appellation of origin, Italian system for the control of quality wine production and counterpart of the French 'Appellation d'Origine Contrôlée'. See also *vino*.

## Denominazione di Origine Controllata e Garantita (DOCG)
Controlled and guaranteed appellation of origin, the highest classification of Italian wines; all aspects of production and maturation are regulated and the wines must be approved by an official tasting panel before being granted the government seal which guarantees authenticity. Only 4 wines qualify at present – *Barolo, Barbaresco, Brunello di Montalcino* and *Vino Nobile di Montepulciano*; Chianti joins with the 1984 harvest.

## Dental
(Liguria) Dentex, sea fish.

## (Al) Dente
'To the tooth'. Firm, cooked to retain some bite or crispness, particularly of pasta and vegetables.

## Dentice
Dentex, Mediterranean fish similar to sea bass.

## Diano d'Alba
(Piemonte) Small town noted for dry red *DOC* wine from *Dolcetto* grapes.

## (Alla) Diavola
Devilled, usually of chicken, split, flattened and grilled; or, of steak and

other ingredients, with a spicy sauce.
*Diavolini*: cheese and cayenne croutons.

## Diavoliccio/diavolillo/diavolino

(Basilicata, Marche, Abruzzo) Hot red pepper, chilli pepper.

## Diego Ralli

Important producers of *Marsala*.

## Diplomatico

Chocolate cake flavoured with rum and coffee. *Diplomatici*: sponge and pastry squares soaked in liqueur.

## Disossato

Boned.

## Ditali(ni)

Tiny pasta tubes, for soup.

## Ditini

(Sicilia) Cinnamon biscuits.

## Ditta

Firm, or business concern.

## DOC(G)

See *Denominazione*.

## Dogliani

(Piemonte) Village known for light red *DOC* wine from *Dolcetto* grapes.

## Dolce

Sweet, mild, soft. Fresh, of water.

*Dolci*: desserts, usually eaten at a pastry shop or cafe rather than in a restaurant; rarely a course in the meal, except on special occasions. *D. di riposto* (Sicilia): sugar-glazed jam pastries. *Dolce torinese*: rich chocolate and almond dessert.

## Dolceacqua

(Liguria) Small town known for dry red *DOC* wine from *Rossese* grapes; local distribution.

## Dolcetto

(Piemonte) Grape variety producing popular, light, fresh red wines, sometimes slightly sparkling; there are 7 *DOC* areas.

## Donnaz

(Valle d'Aosta) Fine red *DOC* wine from *Nebbiolo* grapes.

## Donnici

(Calabria) *DOC* red and rosé wines, mainly from *Gaglioppo* grapes.

## Donzella

Wrasse, sea fish.

## Doppio

Double. Strong, concentrated.

## Dorato

Golden. Glazed. Fried in batter.

## Dormienti

Type of fungus.

## Dorso

Back, e.g. of hare.

## Dragoncello

Tarragon, the herb.

## Drioli

Firm of distillers in Venice, *Veneto*, famous for *Maraschino*.

## (Della) Duchessa

See *tagliatelle*.

## Duja

See *salame*.

## Dunderet

(Piemonte) Boiled potato dumplings, served with cheese or a sauce.

## Dunkel

See *Lagrein*.

## Eisacktaler

See *Valle Isarco*.

## Elba

Napoleon's island. *DOC* for dry red wine from *Sangiovese* grapes and white from *Trebbiano*.

## Elefante di mare

Lobster. See also *piatto*.

## Elicoidali

Ridged curved pasta cylinders.

## Elixir di China

Aperitif/digestive drink containing quinine.

## (All') Emiliana

In the style of *Emilia*. See *tortellini*.

## Enfer d'Arvier

See *Arvier*.

## Enoteca

Wine library, commercial shop or a publicly-funded wine exhibition.

## Erbaggi(o)

Pot herbs, green vegetables, salads.

## Erbaluce

(Piemonte) White grape variety making light dry slightly bitter table wine, and also a rich *Passito* of great endurance.

**Erbazzone**
(Emilia-Romagna) Spinach and cheese pie, sometimes with sugar and almonds; also known as *scarpazzone*.

**Erbe**
Herbs.

**Erbette**
Greens – chard, cabbage, spinach, etc.

**Erbj côn el salam**
(Piemonte) Wild asparagus with sausage and bacon, served with *polenta*.

**Escabecio**
(Abruzzo) Soused, of fish.

**Espresso**
See *caffé*.

**Est! Est!! Est!!! di Montefiascone**
(Lazio) *DOC* wine mainly from *Trebbiano*. So named because a bishop, travelling to Rome in the 12th century, sent his servant ahead to indicate with the sign Est! the hostelleries purveying the best wine; the servant endorsed the wine of Montefiascone with a triple Est!!! and the bishop was sufficiently enthusiastic to abandon his journey and devote the remainder of his days to its consumption, his bones now residing in the local church.

**Estivo**
Of summer.

**Essenza**
Essence, concentrated stock or glaze.

**Etna**
Mountain and *DOC* for red, white and rosé wines.

**Etschtaler**
See *Valdadige*.

## (Alla) Fabrianese

In the style of Fabriano, *Marche*. See *salame, soppressa, trippa*.

## Facciuni di Santa Chiara

(Sicilia) Chocolate-covered almond biscuits.

## Fagianella/fagiano

Pheasant.

## Fagioli

Kidney beans, haricot beans, usually dried. *F. bianci di Spagna*: lima beans. *F. borlotti*: cranberry beans. *F. cannellini*: small white navy beans. *F. freschi*: fresh, not dried, beans. *F. dall'occhio/toscanelli*: black-eyed beans. *F. striati*: striped beans. *F. all'abruzzese*: white beans with ham, tomatoes, hot pepper. *F. al/nel fiascò (Toscana)*: cooked in a flask with oil, garlic and sage. *F. alla fiorentina*: with herbs and egg and lemon sauce. *F. alla gallurese*: with cabbage, fennel, onion, tomato sauce. *F. alla polenta*: pureed with butter and cream. *F. alla romana*: with oil, anchovies and lemon. *F. alla smolz* (Friuli-Venezia Giulia): cranberry beans with bacon, onions, vinegar. *F. all'uccelletto* (Toscana): white beans stewed in oil with tomatoes. *F. zermegai* (Veneto): mixed kinds of beans with pork rinds.
Small short pasta noodles.

## Fagiolini (verdi)

French beans, green beans. *F. all'aretina*: stewed with oil, tomatoes, sage. *F. in fricassea*: with oil, garlic and basil. *F. alla milanese*: with egg, cream, cheese.

## Fagottini

Bundles, rolls, e.g. of veal with a stuffing.

## Faina

(Sardegna, Piemonte, Liguria) Thick pancake of chick pea flour.

## Faiscedda

See *turta*.

## Falerio dei Colli Ascolani

(Marche) Dry white *DOC* wine based on *Trebbiano* grapes; mainly local distribution.

## Falerno

(Lazio, Campania) Dry red non-*DOC* wine made from *Aglianico* grapes.

## Falernum

(Lazio) Light amber-coloured wine from the Cenatiempo winery.

## Falsomagro

See *farsumagru*.

## Famiglioli/famiole

(Piemonte) Type of fungi.

## Familiaro

Homely, simple.

**Fanelli**
Linnets.

**Fanfano/fanfaru**
Pilot fish.

**Fara**
(Piemonte) Red *DOC* wine based on *Nebbiolo* grapes; limited distribution.

**Faraona**
Guinea fowl. *F. alla creta* (Lombardia): roasted in clay.

**Farcito**
Stuffed.

**Farfalle(tte)/farfalloni**
Butterfly-shaped pasta.
(Emilia-Romagna) Small bread rolls.

**Farina**
Flour.

**Farinata (alla ligure)**
Fried cake of chick pea flour. See also *mus*.

**Faro**
(Sicilia) *DOC* zone producing fine but rare red wine from blend of local grape varieties.

**Farricello**
Barley.

**Farro**
See *minestra, su farri*.

**Farsumagru/farsumauru**
(Sicilia) Large slice of beef or veal spread with a rich stuffing of sausage, cheeses, eggs, rolled up and simmered in wine and tomato sauce, served in slices; also known as *falsomagro*.

**Faseui a la tofeja/fasoeil al furn**
(Piemonte) Red haricot beans baked slowly in a special jar in a bread oven with herbs, spices and bacon.

**Fasoi**
(Veneto, Friuli-Venezia Giulia) Beans. *F. e carne salata* (Trentino-Alto Adige): beans with salt beef.

**Fasolare**
(Calabria) Cockles.

## Fasui
(Friuli-Venezia Giulia) Beans.

## Fatto in casa
Homemade.

## (Alla moda del) Fattore.
'Farm-style'. See *anguilla*.

## Fattoria
Farm.

## Favata
(Sardegna) Rich stew of dried beans, pork, fennel, cabbage, tomatoes.

## Fave
Broad beans. *F. 'ngrecce* (Marche): in salad with oil, garlic, marjoram. *F. alla romana*: with bacon, also known as *f. al guanciale* when cooked, correctly, with pork cheek; or stewed in oil with sage. *F. alla trappista* (Sicilia): finished in oil. *F. alla turca*: boiled in the pods.

*Fave dei morti* (Lombardia): almond and pine nut biscuits, traditionally baked for All Soul's Day.

## Favette
(Veneto) Tiny sweet fritters.

## Favolli
Small crabs.

## Fedelini
Very thin pasta noodles, for soup.

## Fegatelli

(Toscana) Small slices, cubes, of pork liver, threaded on skewers with other ingredients. *F. alla bolognese*: marinated with herbs, then grilled. *F. alla fiorentina*: with herbs and spices, wrapped in pig's caul and charcoal grilled or baked. *F. alla petroniana*: baked with bread slices and herbs.

## Fegatini (di pollo)

Chicken livers.

## Fegato

Liver, usually calf's. *F. alla borghese*: larded and marinated, roast. *F. alla contadina*: fried with onion, vinegar, parsley. *F. alla lodigiana*: slices of pork liver wrapped in ham and pig's caul, fried. *F. alla macellara*: sautéed, with lemon and parsley. *F. alla triestina*: studded with cloves, braised, served in slices on toast. *F. alla veneziana*: fried, with onions. *F. alla vicentina*: similar, plus white wine.

## (Di) Felino

Of Felino, *Emilia-Romagna*. See *salame*.

## Fermentazione naturale

Of wine, made sparkling by carbon dioxide released naturally in the fermentation process.

## Fernet-Branca

Dark brown pungent bitters made from herbs, roots and alcohol by Fratelli Branca of Milan, *Lombardia*; used as digestive, aperitif or general pick-me-up.

## (Alla) Ferrarese

In the style of Ferrara, *Emilia-Romagna*. See *gambero, manina*.

## Ferrari

(Trentino-Alto Adige) Company famous for quality sparkling wine.

**(Ai) Ferri**
Grilled.

**Ferro China**
Bitters with high iron and quinine content.

**Fesa**
Leg, of veal.

**Festonati**
Pasta shapes.

**Fetta**
(Sardegna) Salty white sheep's milk cheese.

**Fett(in)e**
Slices, fillets. *F. di pane all'umbra*: slices of bread soaked in oil, lemon, garlic and spread with olives. *(Le) fette* (Toscana): red cabbage soup poured over black bread with garlic.

**Fettuccine**
(Lazio) Long flat ribbons of egg pasta, similar to *tagliatelle* but slightly narrower and more solid. *F. all' Alfredo*: tossed in cream and butter; invented by Alfredo in his Rome restaurant and finished by him with a gold fork and spoon. *F. alla ciociara*: with meat sauce. *F. ricche alla modenese*: with peas, tomatoes, peppers, ham, truffles and cream.

**Fettunta**
(Toscana) Garlic toast.

**Fiadone**
(Abruzzo, Molise) Sweet egg and cheese tart.
*Fiadoni alla trentina*: almond, honey and rum sweetmeats.

**(Alla) Fiamma**
Flambéed.

**Fiandolein**
(Valle d'Aosta) Zabaglione made with rum.

**Fiano**
(Campania) White grape variety.

**(Al) Fiasco**
Cooked in a flask, especially of beans.

**Fica**
Pomfret, sea fish.

**Ficato d'i sette cannoli alla palermitana**
Fried pumpkin with garlic, sugar, vinegar.

**Fichi**
Figs. *F. mandorlati* (Puglia): dried figs flavoured with almonds, fennel seeds and bayleaf.
*Fichi indiani*: prickly pears, fruit.

### (Al) fieno maggengo
See *pitò*.

### Fieto/figa
Pomfret, sea fish.

### Figà
(Veneto) Liver. *F. garbo e dolce*: calf's liver, egg and breadcrumbed, fried, with vinegar and sugar. *F. col radesolo*: pork liver fried with sage.

### Figadini con l'ua
(Veneto) Sautéed chicken livers with grapes.

### Filascetta
(Lombardia) Baked round of yeast dough spread with onions, sugar and cheese.

### Filatelli/filatieddi
(Calabria) Pasta strands, served with cheese and a sauce; also known as *scilatielli*.

### Filato
In strands, threads.

### Filetto
Fillet, of fish. Breast fillet, of chicken, turkey. Fillet, of beef, pork. *F. alla sarda*: of beef, marinated in wine, braised with mushrooms and spices plus anchovy and lemon, served on bread slices. *F. di manzo al sugo signore* (Toscana): beef fillet cooked in milk.

### (Di) Filottrano
See *salsiccia*.

### Finanziera
(Piemonte) Light stew of chicken giblets, sweetbreads, mushrooms, truffles.

### (Alla) Finitese
'Perfect-style'. See *melanne*.

### Finocchio/finocchietti
Fennel, the vegetable and herb.
*Finocchini* (Piemonte): sweet biscuits.

### Finocchiona
(Toscana) Smooth pork sausage flavoured with fennel seeds.

### Finto
Feigned, false. *Finto gnocco*: small pasta shapes.

### Fiocco
(Emilia-Romagna) Shoulder of ham.

### Fiorano
(Lazio) High-quality non-*DOC* wines produced by Prince Boncompagni Ludovisi.

## Fiore

Flower, of e.g. courgette. Floret, of broccoli.

Cheese. *Fior(e) d'alpe* (Lombardia): buttery elastic cheese. *F. di latte: mozzarella* type cheese. *Fiore molle* (Lazio): soft yellow aromatic cheese. *Fiore sardo*: see *pecorino*.

## (Alla) Fiorentina

In the style of Florence, *Toscana*. With spinach, and sometimes cheese sauce, especially of fish. See also *anguilla, asparagi, baccalà, bistecca, fagioli, fegatelli, migliaccio, pasticcio, petto, pisellini, pollo, ravioli, risotto, rognoni, salame, stracotto, strozzapreti, trippa, zucca.*

## Fioroni

Decorative rosettes, of puff pastry etc.

## Fischietti

(Calabria) Homemade macaroni, served with cheese and a sauce; also known as *fusilli, maccarruni i'casa/a firriettu.*

## (Alla) Fiumarola

'River-style'. See *ciriole.*

## Focaccetta

(Liguria) Crisp fritter of pasta dough filled with cheese, usually eaten as a snack; also known as *focaccia.*

## Focaccia

Tart, pie, cake, sweet or savoury. *F. ligure*: baked flat round of yeast dough, with many toppings including herbs, coarse salt, ham, onions, artichokes, cheese; also known as *focaccetta*. See also *sardenaira*. *F. del Venerdì Santo* (Puglia): fennel, endive and anchovy tart with olives and capers; also known as *scalcione.*

## (Sul) Focone
See *roscioli.*

## (Alla) Foggiana
In the style of Foggia, *Puglia*. See *simmuledda, strascinati.*

## Fogher
(Friuli-Venezia Giulia) Hearth, open stove.

## Foglia
Leaf. *F. di lauro*: bayleaf. *F. di vite*: vine leaf.

## Foianeghe
(Trentino) Fine red non-*DOC* wine made in the style of claret from Bordeaux grape varieties by Conte Bossi Fedrigotti.

## Foiolo alla milanese
Tripe and onion stew, with cheese.

## Folaghe
Coot, water fowl. *F. alla Puccini* (Toscana): simmered in white wine, with a sauce of anchovies, smoked salmon, fish roe.

## Fondanti
Small savoury croquettes.

## Fondo
Stock. Heart, bottom, of artichoke.

## Fondue
(Valle d'Aosta) Cheese fondue.

## Fonduta
(Piemonte) *Fontina* cheese fondue with eggs, milk and butter and a final addition of truffles.

## Fongadina
(Veneto) Stewed calf offal and mushrooms, served with *polenta*.

## Fontal
Commercially made version of *fontina* cheese.

## Fontana Candida
Wine company, largest producers of *Frascati*.

## Fontanafredda
Important producer and exporter of wines, based at Serralunga d'Alba, *Piemonte*.

## Fontina
(Piemonte, Valle d'Aosta) Smooth buttery cheese with small holes and delicate fruity flavour, similar to Gruyère, used notably in *fonduta*; made by traditional methods within a legally defined region.

## Forca
See *pesce*.

## Formaggetta
(Piemonte) Small round soft white cheese, sometimes of sheep's milk.

## Formaggio
Cheese; in Italy, the course that follows the salad, often combined with the final fruit course. *F. fresco*: fresh cheese, made locally throughout the country of cow's or sheep's milk or a mixture.

## (Al) Forno/(alla) fornaia
In the oven. Baked, roasted.

## Fragaglie
(Calabria) Tiny red mullet, usually fried whole.

## Fragol(in)e
Strawberries. *F. dei boschi*: wild strawberries.

## Fragolino
Pandora, type of sea bream.
*Fragolino di mare*: curled octopus.

## Francesine
(Lombardia) Long French loaf.

## (Alla) Franceschiello
See *pollo*.

## Franciacorta
(Lombardia) *DOC* region producing still and sparkling white wines from *Pinot* grapes and a blended red.

## Frappato
See *Vittoria*.

**Frappe**
(Lazio) Thin sweet fritters twisted in knots and piled in a pyramid.

**Frascarelli**
(Marche) Small dumplings served in soup.

**Frascati**
(Lazio) Small town and its popular white wine *(DOC)* based on *Malvasia* grapes, nowadays mainly dry but can be semi-sweet or sweet.

**Fratelli**
Brothers.

**Fravioli**
(Sicilia) Fritters filled with *ricotta* cheese.

**Frecciarossa**
Most famous wine estate of *Oltrepo Pavese*.

**Freddo**
Cold.

**Fregnacce**
(Abruzzo, Lazio) Baked pancakes, often stuffed with meat, chicken and cheese.

**Fregolotti**
See *torta*.

**Fregula**
(Sardegna) Saffron flavoured semolina dumplings, cooked in broth with cheese; also known as *succu tundu*.

**Freisa**
(Piemonte) Red grape variety, making wines sometimes dry and biting, sometimes sweet, often with a tendancy to froth.

**Fresa**
See *pane*.

**Fresco**
Fresh, cool.

**Frescobaldi**
Owners of the largest *Chianti* estates.

**Fresse (alla cuneese)**
Fried squares of pig's caul stuffed with pork liver and beef.

**Friarelli**
See *broccoli*.

**Fricassea**
Fricassee, light stew, usually of chicken, veal, lamb, or of mixed vegetables, finished with egg and lemon. See also *fagiolini*.

## Fricc

(Piemonte) Fried cheese and perhaps beaten egg, served with *polenta*.

## Fric(c)o

(Friuli) Fried cake or omelette of cheese, with apples, onions or potatoes.

## Frienno e magnanno

(Campania) Mixture of deep fried foods – fish, veal, offal, cheese, rice, croquettes, courgette flowers etc.

## Friggiona alla modenese

Sliced sausage stewed with onion, tomatoes and peppers.

## Friggitoria

Shop selling fried food.

## Frisceu

(Liguria) Mixed fritters, of fish, calf's brains, mushrooms etc., or of apples, bananas etc.

## Frisedde

(Puglia) Bread softened in water, with tomato, herbs and oil.

## Fritole

(Veneto, Friuli) Fritters, either savoury, of fennel and artichoke hearts, or sweet, with pine nuts and raisins.

## Frittata

Type of omelette cooked slowly on both sides until set and served flat. *F. all'anconetana*: with courgettes and bacon. *F. alla contadina*: with ham and tomatoes. *F. friulana*: soft thick version. *F. genovese*: with spinach. *F. di pasqua alla maniera di Cascia*: with lamb's offal. *F. rognsa* (Piemonte): with meat and sausage. *F. alla savoiarda*: with ham, potatoes, leeks, cheese. *F. fredda alla siciliana*: with cheese, onion, basil, served cold. *F. alla veneta*: with anchovies, garlic, tomatoes.

## Frittatensuppe

(Trentino-Alto Adige) Pancake strips in broth.

## Frittatine

Pancakes. *F. alla lodigiana*: stuffed with slivers of cheese.

## Frittedde

(Sicilia) Vegetable or fruit fritters.

## Frittelle

Fritters. Pancakes. *F. di Giovedì Grasso* (Emilia-Romagna): large sweet pancakes sprinkled with vanilla sugar. *F. di polenta alla lodigiana*: deep fried *polenta* rounds sandwiched with ham, cheese and truffles. *F. di San Giuseppe alla toscana*: rice pancakes with pine nuts and lemon.

## Frittelloni

(Emilia-Romagna) Fried pasta packets stuffed with spinach, raisins and cheese.

## Fritto

Fried. Fried food. *Fritto misto*: mixed fry, comprising various ingredients dipped in batter or egg and breadcrumbs and deep fried, ranging from small veal slices, liver, brains, sweetbreads, kidneys, croquettes, to artichokes, cauliflower, courgettes, mushrooms and with different interpretations throughout the regions of Italy. *F. m. di mare*: mixed fried fish, seafood. *F. m. di verdure*: mixed fried vegetables. *Grande f. m.*: meal consisting entirely of fried dishes – meat, vegetables, cheese, cream and fruit.

*Fritto composto*: mixed fried croquettes, of chicken, ham, tongue etc.

## Frittuli

(Calabria) Fried pork scraps with hot pepper, preserved in salt, as a garnish for soups.

## Frittura

Frying. Fried food. *F. secca alla veneta*: fried croquettes of mixed veal, chicken and sausage.

## Frizon

(Emilia-Romagna) Mixed fried sausage, onion, pepper and tomato.

## Frizzante

Effervescent. Lightly sparkling, of wines.

## Frizze

See *pan*.

## (Alla) Friulana

In the style of *Friuli*. See *agnello, frittata, pollo, salame*.

## Frollo

Tender, high, of meat. Short, of pastry.

## Frullato

Whisked, whipped. *F. di frutta*: fruit whip made with fresh fruit, milk, ice and liqueur.

## Frumento

Wheat.

## Frustingolo/frustingu

(Marche) Fig, raisin and nut cake.

## Frutta/frutti

Fruit, the final course of a meal.

*Frutti di mare*: seafood.

*Frutti di Martorana* (Sicilia)/*fruttini* (Toscana): fruit-shaped almond sweetmeats.

## Fugazza

(Veneto) Rich yeast pastry with orange, spices, almonds.

## Fumetto

Fumet, stock.

## (Al) Funghetto/(a) funghetti

'Mushroom style'. Sautéed with oil, garlic and parsley (but no mushrooms), of vegetables, and sometimes mushrooms themselves.

With mushrooms.

*Funghetti* (Marche): dry mushroom-shaped cakes.

## Funghi

Mushrooms, edible fungi. *F. freschi*: fresh field mushrooms. *F. ovoli/ovuli*: Caesar's mushrooms, imperial agaric. *F. porcini*: cèpes, boletus, often dried. *F. secchi*: dried mushrooms or cèpes. *F. di serra*: cultivated mushrooms. *F. all'ambrosiana* (Lombardia): sautéed with garlic, herbs, wine, lemon and served cold. *F. alla genovese*: fried with potatoes, garlic, basil. *F. alla trasteverina*: fried with anchovies, garlic, tomatoes and mint.

## Fusilli

Spiral spaghetti. *F. alla molisana*: with spicy tomato or lamb sauce. See also *fischietti*.

## Fuso

Melted. Clarified, of butter. Processed, of cheese.

## (In) Gabbia
See *mele*.

## Gabiano
(Piemonte) Small town with a new *DOC* for dry red wine based on *Barbera* grapes.

## Gaglioppo
(Calabria) Red grape variety, known by many local names.

## Galani
(Veneto) Small sweet fritters.

## Galantina
Galantine.

## (In) Galera
See *cotechino*.

## Galestro
(Toscana) Light, dry, non *DOC* white wine, produced by a group of major wine-makers; maximum alcohol content of 10.5°.

## Gallet(in)e
Wafers.

## Galletto
Chicken.

## Galliano
(Lombardia) Bright yellow herby liqueur.

## Gallin(ell)a
Hen, boiling fowl.

## Gallinaci/gallinette
Chanterelles, fungi.

## Gall(inaci)o
Chicken. See also *pesce*.

## Gallura
(Sardegna) *DOC* for dry white wine from *Vermentino* grapes.

## (Alla) Gallurese
In the style of Santa Terese Gallura, *Sardegna*. See *fagioli*.

## Gamay
Red grape variety.

## Gambellara
(Veneto) *DOC* area producing white wines, dry and sweet, based on *Garganega* grapes.

## Gambero (marino)

Lobster.

*Gamber(ell)i*: prawns.

*Gamb(er)etti*: shrimps. *G. alla ferrarese*: simmered in white wine.

*Gamberi d'acqua dolce/di fiume*: freshwater crayfish.

## Gambon

(Emilia-Romagna) Salted pressed ham, served boiled.

## Gancia

Famous wine and vermouth company based in Canelli, *Piemonte*.

## Garagolo(l)i

(Veneto, Marche, Emilia-Romagna) Horn-shells.

## Garganega

(Veneto) White grape variety, basis of *Soave*.

## Garganelli

(Emilia-Romagna) Grooved quill-shaped pasta tubes, homemade with a special instrument; often served with cream and ham.

## Garmucia

(Toscana) Mixed vegetable soup.

## Gelatina

Jelly, aspic.

## Gelato

Frozen, chilled, iced. Ice cream.

## Gelsomino

Jasmine.

## Gemsenfleish

(Trentino-Alto Adige) Chamois cooked in vinegar, served with *polenta*.

## (Alla) Genovese

In the style of Genoa, *Liguria*. With potatoes, garlic, oil and parsley, of fish, meat, mushrooms. With *pesto* sauce, of vegetables. With sauce of meat, ham, onions, of pasta. See also *antipasto, frittata, funghi, lumache, melanzane, minestra, minestrone, moscardini, pesche, polpettone, ravioli, riso, salame, sarde, sardenaira, stecchi, tonno, trippa, vitello.*

*Genovesa/genovese* (Campania): veal or beef larded with bacon, braised with vegetables, served with macaroni.

## Gentile

See *salame*.

## Germano

Mallard.

## Gepökeltes Rindfleish

(Trentino-Alto Adige ) Ham.

## Gerace

See *Bianco*.

## Gerstensuppe

(Trentino-Alto Adige) Barley soup with bacon, onions, celery.

## Gettoni

Token-shaped praline sweets.

## Gewürztraminer

See *Traminer*.

## Ghemme

(Piemonte) Fine red *DOC* wine based on *Nebbiolo* grapes.

## Gherigli

Kernels, of nuts.

## Ghiacci(at)o

Ice, iced.

## Ghiandole

Glands, e.g. of pork.

## (Alla) Ghiotta

'Delicious-style'. Stew of some kind. See also *baccalà, paglia e fieno, palombacci.*

(Calabria, Sicilia) Onions, tomatoes, potatoes, olives, capers, raisins, as the basis for various dishes, especially dried cod, swordfish.

(Abruzzo) Baked peppers, potatoes, courgettes and tomatoes.

`*Ghiotta di pesce* (Sicilia): fish and tomato soup; also known as *zuppa di pesce alla trapanese.*

*Ghiottini* (Toscana): almond biscuits.

## Garofolato

With cloves. *G. di manzo (Lazio): beef, spiked with cloves and slowly braised in tomato sauce.*

## Garofano di mare

Sea anemone.

## Garretto

Shin, of beef.

## Garuzolo

(Veneto) Murex, shellfish.

## Gasse

(Liguria) Small bow shaped pasta, served in broth or with *pesto* sauce.

## Gassificato

Artificially carbonated.

## Gastaurello

Skipper, sea fish.

## Gattò di patate

(Campania) Baked potato cake with ham and cheese.

## Gatto pardo/gattuccio

Dogfish.

## Gavi

(Piemonte) Small town noted for crisp white wine *(DOC)*, from *Cortese* grapes, sometimes sparkling. *G. dei G.*: proprietary *Cortese* wine made by La Scolca; one of Italy's most fashionable dry whites.

## Gefültes Gemüs

(Trentino-Alto Adige) Mixed tomatoes, courgettes, peppers, stuffed with meat and rice.

## Ghiottone

Glutton, gourmand.

## Ghiozzi

Goby, tiny sea fish.

## Ghisau

(Sardegna) Beef stewed with red wine, tomatoes and potatoes; also known as *stuffau.*

**Giallo**
Yellow.

**Giambars**
(Friuli) Crayfish sautéed in oil and garlic, marinated in white wine.

**Giambonetto**
Boned leg of chicken rolled to resemble a ham.

**Gianchetti**
See *bianchetti*.

**Gianchi e neigro**
See *bianco*.

**Giandujotti**
(Piemonte) Nut chocolates.

**Gianfottere**
(Calabria) Stew of aubergines, courgettes, peppers, herbs.

**(Alla) Giardiniera**
'Gardener's style'. Assorted pickled vegetables, sold in jars. See also *minestra*.

**Ginepro**
Juniper berries.

**Ginestrata**
(Toscana) Chicken soup with marsala and spices.

**Gioddu**
(Sardegna) Yoghourt.

**Giovane/giovine**
Young, new.

**Giovedì Grasso**
Shrovetide Thursday. See *frittelle, lasagne*.

**Girò**
(Sardegna) Red grape variety.

## Giromette

(Lombardia) Biscuits in various shapes.

## (Alla) Giudia/giudea

Jewish style. See *carciofi*.

## Giuggiole

Jujube fruits.

## Giuncata

Curds, junket.

## Glassato

Glazed. Iced.

## Gniummerieddi

(Puglia) Lamb or goat innards on skewers, fried or grilled with cheese, bacon and herbs; also known as *gnomirelli, gnumariddi, gnummerieddi*.

## Gnocarei

(Lombardia) Chicken soup with *polenta* squares.

## Gnocchi/gnocco

Small dumplings made with a variety of ingredients – flour, potatoes, semolina, *ricotta* cheese or spinach – usually a first course, occasionally an accompaniment. See also *ciciones, macaroni. Gnocchi alla bava* (Piemonte): of buckwheat, with fresh cheese and cream. *G. alla cadorina* (Veneto): of potato, with butter and smoked *ricotta* cheese. *G. alla cuneese*: of flour, with local cheese and cream. *G. alla molisana*: of potato, with tomato and basil sauce. *G. all'ossolana*: of potato, with meat sauce; or of cheese, with sage. *G. alla piemontese*: of potato, cheese and truffle, with tomato sauce. *G. alla romana*: of semolina and parmesan, a restaurant classic; or of potatoes at home.

*Gnocchi dolci*: sweet dumplings.

*Gnocchetti*: tiny dumplings, for soup. *G. a casce e ova* (Abruzzo): with beaten egg, cheese, bacon.

*Gnocco di pane* (Friuli-Venezia Giulia): steamed bread dumplings, with butter and cheese. *Gnocco fritto* (Emilia-Romagna): pastry fritters served with ham or cheese.

## Gnocculi
(Sicilia) Potato dumplings served with cheese and broth or meat sauce.

## Gnomirelli/gnumariddi/gnummerieddi
See *gniummerieddi*.

## Go
(Veneto) Goby, tiny seafish.

## Gobbi
(Umbria) Cardoons. *G. alla perugina*: fried, with meat sauce.

## Golosessi
See *caramei*.

## Gorgonzola
(Lombardia) Blue veined creamy cheese with strong flavour and smell.

## Governato
On *Chianti* labels indicates use of 'Governo' process – addition of juice from semi-dried grapes to wine fermented in the normal way, bringing about a secondary fermentation and resulting in fresh fruity wine for drinking young.

## Gra Car
(Lombardia) Liqueur made by the Certosa monastery, Pavia – 'Gratium Cartusia', gift of the Carthusians.

## (Alla) Gradese
In the style of the isle of Grado, *Friuli*. See *brodetto*, *seppie*.

## Gradoli
(Lazio) Town known for rare dessert wine *(DOC)*, made from *Aleatico* grapes.

## (Alla) Graela
See *tonno*.

## Gragnano
(Campania) Small town known for fine non-*DOC* red wines.

## Gramigna
Short hollow curved pasta, homemade on a special instrument.

## Gramugia
(Toscana) Artichoke, asparagus, bean and bacon soup.

## Grana
(Lombardia, Emilia-Romagna) Hard close-grained grating cheese similar to parmesan, often with a black coating on the outside.

## Grance(v)ola
Spider crab.

## Granchi/granciporri
Crabs.

**Grande**
Big. Great.

**Granelli**
Grains, seeds, pips.
Testicles, of lamb, calf. *G. alla maremmana*: dipped in flour and egg, fried, with lemon.

**Granita**
(Sicilia) Grainy water ice with frozen crystals, of coffee or fruit, often lemon.

**Grano**
Grain, wheat. *Grano saraceno*: buckwheat. *Granoturco*: sweetcorn.

**Granseola/granze(v)ola**
Spider crab. *G. alla triestina*: baked with breadcrumbs and garlic. *G. alla veneziana*: boiled, served cold with oil and lemon.

**Granzoporro**
(Veneto) Small crab.

**Grappa**
Pungent clear spirit, distillate of the cake left after pressing the grapes in wine-making.

**Grassato/grassatu**
(Sicilia) Goat or lamb stew with potatoes, wine and cheese.

**Grasso**
Fat, rich. With meat, as opposed to meatless. See also *antipasto, polenta*.

**(In) Gratella/(alla/sulla)graticola**
Grilled.

**Gratinato**
Gratinéed, finished in the oven or under the grill for a crisp golden crust, usually with a sprinkling of cheese.

**Grattugiato**
Grated.

**Grave del Friuli**
Large *DOC* region with red and white wines named according to grape variety, 7 authorized types; red *Merlot* predominates.

**Gravioli**
(Abruzzo) Pasta squares stuffed with cheese; also known as *ravioli all'aquilina*.

**(Alla) Greca**
Greek style. Of vegetables, stewed with oil and herbs, served hot or, more often, cold.

**Greco**
Grape variety, both white and black, grown mainly in the south.

## Gremolada/gremolata
Mixture of herbs, garlic and lemon peel sprinkled over *ossobuco* at the end of cooking.

## Grenadine
Small thick nuggets, of veal.

## (Alla) Gricia
(Lazio) With bacon, garlic and hot pepper, of pasta.

## (Al) Grifo
See *cardi*.

## Grifole
Type of fungus which grows on trees.

## (Alla) Griglia
Grilled.

## Grigio
Grey.

## Grignolino
(Piemonte) Grape variety producing light dry delicate red wines.

## Grillettato
Simmered, braised. Fermented, of wine. Braised dish. *G. di vitello alla toscana*: braised veal with wine and ham.

## Grissini (torinese)
Thin sticks of dry bread, universal in Italian restaurants.

## Grive delle Langhe
Pieces of pig's caul stuffed with pork, liver, spices, simmered in oil.

## Grolla
See *caffè*.

**Grongo**
Conger eel.

**Groppa**
Rump, of meat.

**(Alla) Grossetana**
In the style of Grosseto, *Toscana*. With mushroom and tomato sauce, butter and cheese, of pasta. See also *acquacotta, scaveccio*.

**Grosso**
Large, big.

**Gröstl**
(Trentino-Alto Adige) Meat loaf with potatoes and onions.

**Groviera**
(Piemonte, Lombardia) Italian version of Gruyère cheese.

**Grumello**
See *Valtellina*.

**Guanciale**
Cured pork cheek or jowl.

**Guarniziono**
Garnish.

**Guastelle**
(Sicilia) Bread rolls with cheese or meat paste.

**(In) Guazzetto**
See *baccalà, rane*.

**Gubana/gubane**
(Friuli-Venezia Giulia) Light pastry with nuts, raisins, chocolate and *grappa*.

**Gulasch/gulyas**
(Friuli-Venezia Giulia) Beef goulash, with tomatoes, onions, paprika.

**Gurken**
(Trentino-Alto Adige) Gherkins.

**Guscio**
Shell, husk, pod. *Al guscio*: boiled in the shell, of eggs.

**Gussoni**
(Emilia-Romagna) Half-moon pizzas topped with vegetables.

**Gutturnio dei Colli Piacentini**
(Emilia-Romagna) Dry robust red *DOC* wine.

## Hauswurst

(Trentino-Alto Adige) Homemade sausage.

## Hirn-profesen

(Trentino-Alto Adige) Bread slices spread with brains, dipped in batter and fried.

## Imbottigliato (da)

Bottled (by). *I. all'origine*: at the source of production. *I. dal viticoltore*: by the grower. *I. nella zone di produzione*: in the area of production.

## Imbottito

Stuffed.

## Imbrecciata

(Umbria) Chick pea, bean and lentil soup.

## Impanadas

(Sardegna) Meat and vegetable pasties.

## Impanato

Breadcrumbed.

## Impastoiata

(Umbria) Mixed *polenta* and beans finished with tomato sauce.

## Impepata di cozze

(Campania) Mussels cooked in sea water with hot pepper or herbs.

## Incassettato

Encased. See also *lasagna*.

## Indivia (belga)

Belgian endive, chicory.

## Infarinata

(Toscana) *Polenta* cooked with beans, bacon, cabbage, eaten cold or sliced and fried.

**(All') Inferno**
'In hell'. Hotness, spiciness. Or simply, a stew. See also *Valtellina*.

**Infiammato**
Flambéed.

**Inglese**
English. See *salsa, zuppa*.

**Insaccati**
Sausages.

**Insalata**
Salad, either a composite salad, of fish, chicken etc., as a first course, or a simple salad dressed with oil and vinegar, following the main course. *I. alla moda d'Alba*: asparagus, celery and truffles. *I. capricciosa* (Piemonte): strips of celeriac, ham, tongue, with mushrooms and mayonnaise. *I. composta*: composite, elaborate, salad. *I. cotta e cruda*: mixed cooked vegetables and raw salad greens. *I. di mare*: seafood. *I. mista*: mixed. *I. di rinforzo* (Campania): cauliflower with anchovies, capers, olives, 'reinforced' each day with further additions and replacements. *I. russa*: mixed vegetables. *I. siciliana*: stuffed tomatoes and anchovies.

**Insalato**
Salted, salt.

**Insalatina/insalatine**
Salad greens.

**Insalatone**
Mixed salad of cooked vegetables.

**Integrale**
Wholemeal, of bread.

**Interiora**
Offal.

**Intingolo**
Stew, ragoût. Sauce.

**Invecchiato**
Aged, of wines.

**Inverno**
Winter.

**Involtini**
Small rolls or bundles, often of veal or ham slices, wrapped round a stuffing and braised.

**Iota**
See *jota*.

**I Piani**
(Sardegna) Popular branded red wine made by *Sella & Mosca*.

### (All') Ischiana
In the style of the isle of Ischia, *Campania*. See *coniglio*.

### Is longus
(Sardegna) Grilled or spit-roasted intestines, of ox, cow.

### Ischia
(Campania) Island and *DOC* for red and white wines, mostly consumed locally.

### Isonzo
(Friuli) *DOC* region with 10 types of wine authorized, named according to grape variety; especially noted for reds.

### (D') Ivrea
Of Ivrea, *Piemonte*. See *polenta*.

## Jaccoli

(Lazio) Thick spaghetti, served with meat sauce and cheese; also known as *maccheroni a fezze*.

## Jerzu

(Sardegna) Village and its wine made by local cooperative.

## Jota

(Friuli-Venezia Giulia) Bean, turnip and *polenta* soup; or bean, potato, sauerkraut and bacon soup.

**Kaiserfleish**
(Trentino-Alto Adige) Smoked pork, served with sauerkraut.

**Kalterersee**
See *Caldaro*.

**Kaminwurz**
(Trentino-Alto Adige) Small smoked sausages.

**Kanostrelle**
(Valle d'Aosta) Ring-shaped cakes with whipped cream.

**Kastanientorte**
(Trentino-Alto Adige) Sweet chestnut cake with cream.

**Knöd(e)l**
Large round dumplings, of breadcrumbs, rye or buckwheat flour, with various added ingredients. *K. alla tirolese in brodo*: made with bread and bacon, in beef broth.

**Knolle**
(Valle d'Aosta) Large boiled dumplings.

**Krapfen**
(Trentino-Alto Adige) Sweet fritters.

**Krenfleish**
(Trentino-Alto Adige) Boiled pork with vinegar and wine, served with horseradish and potatoes.

**Kretzer**
See *Lagrein*.

**Laccetto/lacerto**
Mackerel.

**Laccie**
Freshwater fish.

**Lacryma Christi del Vesuvio**
(Campania) Red, rosé and white wines, the latter either dry, sweet, fortified or sparkling, grown around Mount Vesuvius; the only ones recognized for *DOC*, although several wines are sold under the name *Lacryma Cristi* ('Tear of Christ').

**Lagana(edd)e/laganelle**
(Calabria, Puglia, Molise, Sardegna) Pasta sheets or strips, often served with butter, cheese and hot pepper.

**Lago di Caldaro**
See *Caldaro*.

**Lagrein**
(Alto Adige) Red grape variety. *L. rosato*: rosé wine made from *Lagrein*; also known as *Kretzer*. *L. scuro*: red *Lagrein* wine; also known as *Dunkel*.

**Lambrusco**
(Emilia-Romagna) Family of grape varieties with branches known as Grasparossa and Salamino, producing light red, dry or sweet, naturally sparkling wines, with *DOC* in 4 areas, Castelvetre, Reggio, Santo Croce and Sorbara; exported in large quantities.

**Lamezia**
(Calabria) Dry red wine *(DOC)*.

**(Alla) Lamonese**
In the style of Lamon, *Veneto*. See *riso*.

**(Alla) Lampada**
Cooked at your table over an individual stove.

**Lampascioni/lampasinoli**
See *cipiduzzi*.

**Lamponi**
Raspberries.

**Lampreda (marina)**
Sea lamprey, similar to eel.

**Lampuga**
Dolphin fish.

**Langhe**
(Piemonte) Important wine-growing region near Alba. See also *grive*, *lasagna*.

**Lanzado**
Mackerel.

## Lardo
Salt pork. *Lardoncini*: fried cubes of salt pork, lardoons.

## (Alla) Lariana
In the style of Lake Como or Lario. See *tinca*.

## Lasagna/lasagne
Strips or sheets of egg pasta, often coloured green with spinach *(l. verde)* and usually layered with other ingredients and finished in the oven. *L. alla bolognese*: the classic interpretation, with meat sauce, béchamel and parmesan. *L. da fornel* (Veneto): with a sauce of nuts, raisins, apples, figs. *L. alla maniera delle Langhe albesi*: with mutton sweetbreads and kidneys, sausage, pig's blood. *L. incassettata alla marchigiana*: with meat, chicken giblet and truffle sauce. *L. napoletana*: with a sauce from braised ham or pork (following as a second course) and *ricotta* cheese; also known as *L. di Giovedì Grasso*. *L. imbottita/pasticciata alla napoletana*: with meat sauce, sausage, hard-boiled eggs, cheese; also known as *l. di Carnevale*. *L. al papavero* (Friuli-Venezia Giulia): with butter, sugar and poppy seeds. *L. in foglia alla maniera di Ragusa*: with veal, cheese and tomato sauce.

*Lasagnette*: pasta ribbons. *L. alla catanese*: with tomato sauce, peppers, anchovies, olives.

## Lasca
Roach, freshwater fish.

## Latisana
(Friuli) *DOC* wine zone; 7 types authorized and named according to grape variety.

## Lattaiolo
(Marche, Toscana) Baked milk pudding.

## Latte
Milk. *L. brusco* (Liguria): custard fritters.

**Latterini**
Sand smelt, small fish.

**Latticino**
(Abruzzo) Fresh mountain cheese.

**Lattuga**
Lettuce. *L. a cappuccio*: round lettuce. *L. romana*: cos lettuce.

**Lauro**
Bayleaf.

**Lavarello**
Salmon-type fish from Lake Como; also known as *coregone*.

**Leberknodel**
(Friuli) Liver dumplings.

**(Alla) Leccese**
In the style of Lecce, *Puglia*. See *cozze, salsiccia*.

**Leccia**
Pompano, sea fish; or amberjack.

**Lenti(cchie)**
Lentils. *L. alla romagnola*: with oil, tomatoes and garlic.

**Lepre**
Hare. *L. alla boema* (Friuli-Venezia Giulia): in a stew finished with vinegar and sugar. *L. crostata* (Lombardia): spit-roasted, baked with cream and covered in almond paste. *L. alla montanura*: stewed in red wine with pine nuts and sultanas. *L. al sivè* (Piemonte): jugged – marinated in red wine, then stewed with the blood added. *L. alla trentina*: marinated and stewed in herbs and wine, plus spices, nuts, raisins, and served with *polenta*. *L. alla vignarola* (Piemonte): marinated and stewed with white wine, grapes, herbs and spices.

**Lepudrida**
(Sardegna) Rich meat and vegetable soup.

**Less(at)o**
Boiled, stewed. Boiled meat. *L. valdostano*: meat and sausage boiled in a sealed pot.

**Lessona**
(Piemonte) Red *DOC* wine based on *Nebbiolo* grapes; limited distribution.

**Letterato**
Small tuna fish.

**Leverano**
(Puglia) Red, white and rosé wines *(DOC)*.

## Licurdia
(Calabria) Potato and onion soup with bread and hot pepper; also known as *brodetto vegetale*.

## Lievero
Leveret, small hare.

## Lievito
Yeast. *Lievitato*: leavened, with yeast.

## (Alla) Ligure
In the style of *Liguria*. See *datteri, farinata, focaccia, lumache, sarde, stecchi.*

## Limone
Lemon. *Al limone*: sautéed and finished with lemon juice, of meat. *L. spremuta*: fresh lemon juice with sugar and ice.

*Limonata*: lemonade.

*Limone di mare*: small sea creature, the French 'violet', whose yellow inside is eaten raw; also known as *mammello di vacca* and *uovo di mare*.

## (Alla) Limonese
In the style of Limone, *Piemonte*. See *cannelloni, capretto*.

## Lingua
Tongue. *L. di bue alla borghese*: braised ox tongue with wine, brandy and salt pork.

*Lingue di gatto* (Piemonte): 'cat's tongues', long thin biscuits.

## Linguattola
Small flat sea fish.

## Lingu(in)e (di passera)
Long flat pasta noodles ('sparrow's tongues').

## Lipari
(Sicilia) Group of islands producing dessert wines *(DOC)* based on *Malvasia* grapes.

## Liquoroso
Wine of high strength, most often fortified by the addition of alcohol.

## Liscio
Smooth.

## Lison
(Veneto) Small town making dry white *DOC* wine from *Tocai* grapes.

## Lissa
(Veneto) Pompano, sea fish.

## Lista
Menu.

## (Alla) Livornese
In the style of Livorno, *Toscana*. With tomato sauce, especially of fish and shellfish. See also *cacciucco, cuscusu, scaloppine*.

## Locorotondo
(Puglia) Light dry white *DOC* wine with a good local reputation.

## (Alla) Lodigiana
In the style of Lodi, *Lombardia*. See *fegato, frittatine, frittelle, polenta*.
*Lodigiano/lodi grana*: piquant local variety of *grana* cheese.

## Lodole
Larks.

## (Alla) Lombarda
In the style of *Lombardia*. See *manzo*.

## Lombata/lomb(ell)o
Loin of pork. Sirloin, of beef. Loin, back, of rabbit. T-bone, of veal. *Lombo di maiale al latte* (Marche): pork loin studded with cloves and cinnamon, braised in milk.
*Lombatina/lombatino*: entrecôte steak, of beef; loin chop.

## Lonza
Fillet of pork cured with spices and wine, eaten raw in thin slices.
Loin, often of pork. *L. di maiale alla perugina*: pork roasted with garlic.

## Lotregan
(Veneto) Grey mullet.

## Lotture
(Sardegna) Type of bread.

## Lucanega/lucanica/lucaniga
(Lombardia, Veneto) Mild pork sausage with parmesan and spice; often cooked in white wine, with rice, or grilled; also known as *luganega, lujanie*.

## (Alla) Lucchese
In the style of Lucca, *Toscana*. See *trippa*.

## Luccio

Pike, freshwater fish. *L. del Trasimeno arrostito*: larded with baccon and anchovies and roast, with piquant mayonnaise.
*Luccio marino*: barracuda.

## Lucertola

See *pesce*.

## (Alla) Luciana

In the style of Santa Lucia in Naples, *Campania*. See *polpo*.

## Lugana

(Veneto) Small town known for fine dry white *DOC* wine based on *Trebbiano*.

## Luganega/lujanie

See *lucanega*.

## Lumache

Snails. *L. alla bobbiese*: simmered with leeks and wine. *L. alla castellana* (Lombardia): with frogs' legs, white wine and truffles. *L. alla genovese/alla ligure*: sautéed, with lemon. *L. alla meranese*: stewed with bacon and wine, plus peas. *L. all'ossolana*: baked in the shells, stuffed with macaroons and nuts. *L. alla piemontese*: fried with onions, served with lemon. *L. alla romana*: stewed with tomatoes, anchovy, mint, hot pepper.
*Lumach(ell)e*: pasta shells.

## Lümasse e saôtissa a la côneeisa

(Piemonte) Snails and sausage cooked in wine, served with *polenta*.

## Lupini

(Emilia-Romagna) Little round sweets.

### Luppoli
Hops.

### Lustro
(Calabria) Grey mullet.

### Luvasu
(Sicilia) Pandora, sea bream.

### Luxardo
Important firm of distillers based in Padua, *Veneto*.

### Luxerna
(Liguria) Grouper, sea fish.

### Macarones caidos
See *ciciones*.

### Macaroni alla veronese
Potato dumplings, served with parmesan and butter.

### Macc
See *al macc*.

### Maccarello
(Lazio) Mackerel.

### Maccarese
(Lazio) Large state-owned agricultural and wine-making estate near Rome; its best wine is the red Castel San Giorgio Reserva.

### Maccar(r)ones (a ferritus)
(Sardegna) Small pasta cylinders made with a special instrument ('ferritu'), served with *ricotta* cheese or meat or tomato sauce.

### Maccarruni (di casa)/maccheruna
(Sicilia) Pasta strips, served with a rich sauce of meat balls, sausage and chicken, or layered with pork, ham and tomato sauce and finished in the oven. See also *fischietti*.

### Maccheroni
Macaroni, thick pasta tubes. See also *jaccoli*. *M. alla maniera di Andria*: with tomato and rue sauce. *M. alla ciociara*: with ham and sausage. *M. alla pastora* (Calabria): with *ricotta* cheese, butter and pepper, or with pork and smoked cheese. *M. saltati* (Calabria): with a rich sauce of meat, poultry and game. *M. alla San Giovanniello* (Campania): with ham, tomato and basil sauce.

*Maccheroni alla chitarra* (Abruzzo, Molise): thin pasta noodles, square in cross-section, cut on a special loom with strings like a guitar; usually served with meat and spicy tomato sauce.

*Maccheroncelli/maccheroncini*: small short macaroni, often ridged. *M. alla Saffi* (Lazio): with asparagus, ham and cream; named after a 19th-century governor of Rome.

**Macco/maccu**
(Sicilia) Mush of boiled beans with oil and wild fennel.

**(Alla) Macedone/macedonia**
Fruit salad. Mixed vegetables.

**(Alla) Macellara**
'Butcher's style'. See *fegato*.
*Macelleria*: butcher's shop.

**(Alla) Maceratese**
In the style of Macerata, *Marche*. See *piselli*.

**Mach**
(Lombardia) Milk, rice and chestnut soup.

**Machet**
(Piemonte) *Polenta* with milk and chestnuts.

**Machitt**
(Lombardia) Boiled turnips, cabbage and beans.

**Macinato**
Ground, pounded, minced.

**Macis**
Mace, the spice.

**Maddalene**
Madeleines, small shell-shaped cakes.

**Mafalde**
Long pasta strips with crimped edges.

**Magasso**
(Veneto) Wild duck.

**Maggiorana**
Marjoram, the herb.

**Maggiore**
Greater, larger.

**Magnonese**
(Veneto) Warm mayonnaise sauce, served with fish and boiled meat.

**Magnosa**
Flat lobster.

**Magro**
Thin, lean. Meatless, applied to a dish for fast days.

**Maiale**
Pork. *M. ubriaco* (Toscana): 'tipsy' pork chops cooked in red wine.
*Maialino*: sucking pig.

**Maionese**
Mayonnaise.

**Mais**
Maize.

**Malbec**
Red grape variety, native of Bordeaux, grown widely in the north.

**Malfatti**
(Lombardia) Spinach and cheese dumplings.

**Malloreddus**
See *ciciones.*

**Maltagliati/maltajà**
(Emilia, Lombardia, Veneto) Short triangular, square or quill-shaped pasta noodles.
*Maltajà* (Lombardia): thick bean and vegetable soup with bacon and pasta.

**Malterrata**
See *mandorle.*

**Malva**
Mallow, plant.

**Malvasia**
Family of grape varieties originating in Greece, now grown throughout the world; in Italy the name is applied to many types which contribute many different styles of wine.

**Mamertino**
(Sicilia) Light golden dessert wine, fairly rare; one of the oldest wine names of the island.

**Mammella**
Udder, of cow. See also *limone.*

## Mammole
(Lazio) Artichokes.

## Mandarini
Mandarins. Tangerines.

## Mandilli de sèa
(Liguria) Delicate pasta squares (like a 'silk handkerchief'), served with *pesto* sauce.

## Mandorle
Almonds.

## Mandorlato/mandorlata:
Almond cake or sweet, nougat; also known as *malterrata*. With almonds. *Mandorlata di peperoni* (Basilicata): stewed peppers and tomatoes with almonds.

## Mandovo
(Marche) Almond confection.

## Mandrolisai
(Sardegna) Full-bodied red and rosé *DOC* wines.

## Manduria
(Puglia) Town producing strong red wine *(DOC)* made from *Primitivo* grapes; may be dry or sweet and sometimes fortified.

## Manfrigul
(Romagna) Tiny pasta nuggets, for soup.

**Manicotto**
(Emilia-Romagna) Creamy pork sausage, served boiled.

**(Alla) Maniera di**
In the style of.

**Manina ferrarese**
Crisp bread roll in a double horseshoe shape.

**(A) mannella**
See *melanzane*.

**Mantecato**
Softened, pounded.

**Manteche**
See *burrino*.

**Mantede**
(Campania) Type of cheese.

**(Alla) Mantovana**
In the style of Mantua, *Lombardia*. See *risotto, turtei, valigini*.
*Mantovana*: fat oblong loaf.

**Manzo**
Beef, technically from an animal under 4 years old. *M. alla California* (Lombardia): braised in vinegar, broth and cream. *M. alla certosina*: stewed with bacon, anchovies and herbs. *M. brasato alla lombarda*: lengthily cooked in red wine. *M. lessato alla piemontese*: boiled beef reheated with tomato sauce and cardoons. *M. alla sarda*: braised in white wine. *M. alla trentina/vecchia Trento*: stewed with vinegar and cream.

**Mappina**
(Calabria) Substantial prepared salad.

**Marai**
(Lombardia) Borage, the herb.

**Marasche**
Morello cherries.

**Maraschino**
Cherry liqueur.

**Marcetto**
(Abruzzo) Mouldy *pecorino* cheese macerated in sheep's milk.

**(Alla) marchigiana**
In the style of *Marche*. See *lasagna, moscardini, nasello, rattatuia, saltimbocca, sarde, trippa*.

**Marchio depositato**
Registered trade name, mark.

**Mare**
Sea.

**(Alla) Maremmana**
In the style of the Maremma region, *Toscana*. See *granelli*.

**Margherita**
See *pizza, torta*.

**Mariconde**
(Lombardia) Small bread and cheese dumplings cooked in broth.

**(Alla) Marinara**
'Sailor's style'. With seafood, e.g. of rice. With tomato sauce and hot red pepper, perhaps garlic, capers, olives, of pasta. Simmered with oil, wine, parsley and garlic, of shellfish. See also *caponata, pizza, triglie*.

**Marinato**
Marinated. Marinated, soused dish.

**Marino**
(Lazio) Small town making *DOC* white wine similar to *Frascati*; mostly dry, though may be sweet or sparkling.
Marine, of the sea.

**Maritato**
See *minestra*.

**Maritozzi**
(Lazio) Raisin and nut buns.

**Marmellata**
Preserve, paste, jam.

**Marmitta**
Cooking pot, saucepan. *M. torinese*: potato and vegetable soup, poured over slices of bread with parmesan.

**Marmora**
Striped sea bream.

**Marò**
(Liguria) Pounded beans with mint, garlic, oil and cheese, to accompany boiled meats; also known as *pestun de fave*.

**Marsala**
(Sicilia) Famous fortified dessert wine *(DOC)*, from the town of that name, sold in various categories according to age: *fine*: 17°, aged 4 months; *superiore*: 18°, aged 2 years; *vergine*: 18°, aged 5 years; *speciale*: 18°, aged 6 months (not a *DOC* category); *all'uovo*: with the addition of egg yolks, ranging from dry to sweet.

**Martello**
See *pesce*.

## Martina Franca
(Puglia) Light dry white *DOC* wine.

## Martini & Rossi
World-famous wine and vermouth company, based in Turin, *Piemonte.*

## Marubini
(Lombardia) Pasta rounds stuffed with beef marrow and cheese.

## Marzapane
(Piemonte) Spicy blood pudding, boiled, baked or fried in slices. *Marzapani*: marzipan sweets.

## Marzemino
(Trentino, Lombardia) Red grape variety.

## Masanette
(Veneto) Female shore crabs with the shells.

## Mascarpone/mascherpone
(Lombardia) Unsalted delicate white cream cheese, wrapped in muslin and to be eaten immediately; often sweetened and whipped up with liqueurs as a dessert.

## Masculini
(Sicilia) Tiny anchovies, often served with spaghetti.

## Masi
(Veneto) Company known for quality wines.

## Mastroberadino
(Campania) Company famous for *Taurasi* and other wines.

## Mataloc
(Lombardia) Fruit and nut cake.

## Matelica
(Marche) Dry white *DOC* wine from *Verdicchio* grapes.

## Matino
(Puglia) Red and rosé *DOC* wines based on *Negroamaro* grapes.

## (Alla) Matticella
See *carciofi*.

## Mazaro
(Veneto) Mallard. *M. a la valesana:* marinated in vinegar, roast and finished with anchovies ('of the peach valleys').

## Mazzafegato
(Marche, Umbria) Pork liver sausage with spices and sometimes raisins and pine nuts.

## Mazzancuogni/mazzancelle/mazzancolle
Large prawns.

## Mazzarelle d'agnello
(Molise) Lamb's offal wrapped in greens, cooked in oil and wine.

## Medaglione
Tournedos, thick slice, of veal.

## Meiroun 'd crava
(Piemonte) Boiled salted or smoked goat.

## Melagrane
Pomegranates.

## Melanzane

Aubergines, egg plants. *M. a ventaglio alla catanese*: spread out in a fan shape and fried. *M. alla finitese* (Calabria): stuffed with cheese, basil, hot pepper and deep fried. *M. alla genovese*: stewed with oil and tomatoes, plus beaten egg. *M. a mannella* (Campania): fried, then layered with cheese, tomatoes, vinegar and finished in the oven. *M. a polpetta* (Calabria): stewed with eggs and garlic. *M. alla rossanese*: cold, dressed with vinegar, garlic etc. *M. imbottite alla siciliana*: stuffed with sardines, cheese, capers.

## Mele

Apples. *M. alla certosa*: baked stuffed apples. *M. in gabbia*: apple dumplings ('in a cage').

## Melissa

(Calabria) Red and white *DOC* wines.

## Melu

Blue whiting.

## Mennola

Picarel, type of sea bream.

## Menta

Mint, the herb. *Menta peperina/romana/mentuccia*: peppermint.

## Mentuccia

Mint-flavoured liqueur.

## Meraner (Husel)/Meranese (di Collina)

(Alto Adige) Light red *DOC* wine based on *Schiava* grapes.

## (Alla) Meranese

In the style of Merano, *Trentino-Alto Adige*. See *lumache*.

## Merca

(Sardegna) Grey mullet boiled in salt water and rolled into a sausage with herbs.

## Mercandele

(Friuli- Venezia Giulia) Fried meat balls of pork and liver.

## Merenda

Snack, light meal, tea.

## Meringhe

Meringues. *Meringato*: with meringue.

## Merlano

Whiting.

## Merlo

Blackbird.
*Merlo marino*: wrasse, sea fish.

### Merlot
Red grape variety, native of Bordeaux, grown widely in the northeast for light dry fruity wines.

### Merluzzo
Cod, hake, whiting. *M. cappellano*: poor cod.

### Mesciua
(Liguria) Chick pea, bean and wheat soup.

### Messicani
(Lombardia) Rolled veal escalopes stuffed with ham or sausage and cheese, fried and finished with wine.

### (Alla) Messinese
In the style of Messina, *Sicilia*. See *pescestocco*.

### Mesta
(Friuli-Venezia Giulia) *Polenta* with cold milk.

### Metaponto
(Basilicata) Small town with cooperative making popular local wines.

### Metauro
(Marche) *DOC* area for light dry white wine made from *Bianchello* grapes.

### Methodo champenois
Of sparkling wine, made by the Champagne method of fermentation in bottle.

### Mezzani
Pasta tubes; also known as *mezzi rigatoni* when ridged.

### Mezze penne
Short quills of pasta.

### Mezze ziti/mezza zita
Long thick pasta tubes.

### Mezzo
Half, semi.

### Miascia
(Lombardia) Baked bread pudding with apples, pears, raisins, herbs.

## Miccone
See *pavese*.

## Michetta
(Lombardia, Veneto, Sicilia) Round bread roll; also known as *rosetta*.

## Midolla
Crumb, of a loaf. Pulp, flesh, of fruit.
*Midollo*: bone marrow.

## Miele
Honey.

## Migliaccio
(Umbria, Marche, Emilia-Romagna, Puglia, Toscana) Pork blood mixed variously with nuts, spices, raisins, honey etc. and fried as a flat cake or baked as a tart; also known in *Toscana* as *sanguinaccio alla fiorentina*.

## Migliulatello
See *cazmarr*.

## Mignuic/mignule
(Puglia, Sicilia) Pasta curls served with various sauces and cheese; also known as *cavatieddi*.

## (Alla) Milanese
In the style of Milan, *Lombardia*. Coated with egg and breadcrumbs, fried in butter and finished with lemon, of veal cutlets and escalopes, liver, ham, fish, vegetables. With rice. See also *asparagi, cardi, fagiolini, foiolo, minestrone, mozzarella, risotto, salame, spinaci, verzata*.

## Millassata
(Sicilia) Cheese omelette with artichokes and asparagus.

## Millefiore
Gold-coloured liqueur, said to contain the extracts of 'a thousand flowers'.

## Millescosedde
(Calabria) Vegetable and pasta soup.

## Mille foglie
Flaky pastry.

## Milza
Spleen. *M. di bue alla monticiana*: fried ox spleen with herbs and anchovies.

## Milzschnittensuppe
(Trentino-Alto Adige) Beef broth with fried bread spread with spleen, eggs and garlic.

## Minerale
Mineral water.

## Minestra

First course of a meal, after the *antipasto*, either soup or pasta, rice, dumplings or similar. *M. asciutta*: 'dry', eaten with a fork, not a spoon, i.e. pasta etc. *M. in brodo*: pasta or rice etc. cooked in broth, or soup with starchy addition. *M. col battuto alla romana*: pasta soup with ham fat, onions, garlic. *M. di bavette alla genovese*: pasta soup with broth from the *cima*. *M. carsolina*: beaten egg with flour fried, then boiled in broth. *M. di farro* (Umbria): semolina soup with tomatoes, onions. *M. giardiniera* (Piemonte): mixed vegetable soup. *M. maritata* (Campania): substantial soup, based on cabbage, ham, sausage; also known as *pignato grosso*. *M. maritata* (Puglia): fennel, celery, escarole etc. layered with cheese, bacon and broth and baked. *M. di riso alla cappuccina*: thick rice soup with pounded anchovies.

## Minestrina

Soup, light broth. *M. tricolore*: potato soup with carrots and parsley.

## Minestrone

Substantial thick soup of mixed vegetables with a starchy addition of pasta, rice, beans or potatoes, in countless local versions. *M. alla genovese*: elaborate mix of vegetables and pasta, with *pesto* sauce. *M. alla milanese*: the classic version, tomatoes, peas, beans, courgettes, potatoes, cabbage, with bacon and rice; often served at room temperature (*semi-freddo*) or as a cold soup in summer. *M. alla novarese*: including red cabbage and cranberry beans. *M. alla sarda*: beans, chick peas, potatoes, cabbage, fennel, pork and pasta. *M. teramano*: green vegetables, pork rinds and meat balls. *M. alla toscana*: beans, escarole, tomatoes and pasta.

## Minnich(i)/minuich

(Basilicata) Homemade pasta tubes, often served with cabbage.

## Miroton di bue

(Piemonte) Boiled beef sliced and assembled with rice, tomatoes, cheese sauce and the broth.

## Mirtilli

Bilberries, blueberries.

## Mirto

Myrtle, the herb, used especially in *Sardegna*.

## Misoltini/missoltitt

See *agoni*.

## Misticanza

(Marche, Lazio, Umbria) Salad of chicory, endive, cress, rocket and other wild greens.

## Misto

Mixed. *M. griglia*: mixed grill. *M. mare*: mixed fried seafood.

## Mitili

Mussels.

**Mitona**
See *zuppa*.

**Mocetta**
(Valle d'Aosta) Dried salted chamois or goat, served thinly sliced as a first course.

**(Alla) Moda di**
In the style of.

**(Alla) Modenese**
In the style of Modena, *Emilia-Romagna*. See *bocconcini, costolette, fettuccine, friggiona, tortellini.*

**Mohnnudeln**
(Friuli-Venezia Giulia) Boiled pasta strips with butter, sugar and poppy seeds.

**Moleche**
(Veneto) Shore crabs without the shell, considered a delicacy. *M. alla muranese*: coated in egg and flour and fried.

**(Alla) Molisana**
In the style of *Molise*. See *fusilli, gnocchi, taralli.*

**Moliterno**
(Calabria, Basilicata) Type of cheese.

**Molle(tto)**
Soft. Soft-boiled, of eggs.

**Mollica (di pane)**
Crumb, of bread.

**Molluschi**
Molluscs.

## Molva occhiona
Mediterranean ling, similar to whiting.

## Monachini
Bullfinch.

## Mondeghili
(Lombardia) Meat balls made with beef and cheese, egg-and-breadcrumbed and fried.

## Monferrato
(Piemonte) *DOC* zone for red and white wines named according to grape variety.

## Monica
(Sardegna) Red grape variety.

## Montalcino
(Toscana) Town renowned for *Brunello di M. (DOCG)*, one of the country's most prestigious red wines; made from *Sangiovese* Grosso grapes (known locally as *Brunello*), it must have 12.5° alcohol and a minimum of 4 years ageing in wood, and may be called *riserva* after 5 years. *Rosso di M. (DOC)*: lighter fresher red wine from the same grape variety. The foremost name is *Biondi-Santi*, the first to make *Brunello* about a century ago, but the area also houses one of Europe's largest wineries, built by the American company Villa Banfi.

## (Alla) Montanara
'Mountain-style'. See *trippa*.

## (Alla) Montanura
See *lepre*.

## Montasio
(Veneto) Smooth firm mild cheese, hard and sharp when matured, similar to *asiago*.

## Montasù
(Piemonte, Lombardia, Emilia-Romagna) Solid triangular bread loaf.

## Montato
Whipped, of cream.

## Monte bianco
Chestnut dessert topped with cream (like Mont Blanc).

## Montecarlo
(Toscana) Fine dry white *DOC* wine based on *Trebbiano* grapes.

## Montecompatri Colonna
(Lazio) *DOC* area producing dry and sweet white wines based on *Malvasia*; mainly local distribution.

## Montefalco
(Umbria) Town known for red *DOC* wines, sometimes dry, can be slightly sweet and slightly sparkling. *M. rosso*: based on *Sangiovese*. *Sagrantino di M.*: deep-coloured robust wine made from semi-dried grapes.

## (Del) Montefeltro
Of the Montefeltro region, *Marche*. See *costolette, prosciutto*.

## Montefiascone
See *Est! Est!! Est!!!*

## Montello e Colli Asolani
(Veneto) *DOC* wine region, with 3 authorized types named according to grape variety.

## Montepulciano
(Toscana) Town famous for *vino nobile di M.*, one of Italy's best red wines *(DOCG)*, based on *Sangiovese* Grosso. It must have a minimum of 12° alcohol, and 2 years ageing; after 3 years it may be called *riserva*, after 4 years *riserva speciale*.

(Abruzzo) Red grape variety.

## Monterosso Val d'Arda
(Emilia-Romagna) White *DOC* wine based on *Malvasia* grapes; mainly dry but can be semi-sweet and sparkling.

## Montescudaio
(Toscana) Red and white *DOC* wines.

## (Alla) Monticiana
See *baccalà, milza*.

## Montone
Mutton.

## (Alla) Monzese
In the style of Monza, *Lombardia*. See *risotto*.

## Monzittas

(Sardegna) Snails. *M. alla maniera di Sassari*: deep fried, with garlic, herbs, lemon.

## Morbidelle

Tiny dumplings, for soup.

## Morellino di Scansano

(Toscana) Red *DOC* wine based on *Sangiovese* grapes.

## Morena

Sea eel, lamprey.

## Morgex

See *Blanc*.

## Moriglione

Wild duck, found especially in the Po valley.

## Morseddu/morzeddu

See *murseddu*.

## Mortadella

(Emilia-Romagna) Huge smooth pork sausage flavoured with coriander and white wine, distinctively speckled inside, usually sliced finely and eaten cold; the famous product of Bologna.

(Abruzzo) *Mortadella fegato dolce/pazzo*: liver sausage with honey, orange, nuts, or with hot pepper. *M. di Campotosto*: small smooth sausage with a cylinder of bacon inside.

## Moscardini

Small curled octopuses. *M. alla genovese*: stewed with herbs, tomatoes, mushrooms. *M. alla marchigiana*: stewed with anchovies and hot pepper.

## Moscato

Muscat, muscatel. See also *noce*.

Family of grape varieties, grown throughout the country and producing wines varying from light to heavy, slightly to very sweet, still to fully sparkling, all with a very characteristic aroma.

## Mosciame

See *musciame*.

## Moscovita

Moulded rich dessert mousse.

## (Alla) Mosiana

See *stecchi*.

## Moscioli

(Marche) Mussels.

## Mostaccioli

(Emilia-Romagna, Abruzzo, Calabria, Sicilia) Cakes or biscuits with various ingredients – candied fruit, almonds, honey, grape must, in

different shapes; also known as *mustazzoli*.
Quill-shaped pasta.

## Mostarda

Preserve, paste. *M. di Cremona/di frutta*: preserved cherries, figs, pears etc., with mustard, honey, white wine, eaten with boiled meats.
(Sicilia) Dried sweetmeat of grape must or prickly pear juice.

## Mosto

Grape must, unfermented grape juice.

## Motella

Three-beard rockling, Mediterranean fish.

## Mozzarella

(Campania, Lazio) Pure white elastic cheese with bland slightly sour flavour, stored in water and used dripping fresh, as a first course and in cooking, especially for pizza. Originally of water buffalo's milk, which is still produced in the south and also known as *bufalina*, but now made of cow's milk throughout Italy, available in different shapes, fresh or smoked. *M. in carrozza*: in a bread sandwich ('carriage'), fried. *M. milanese*: dipped in egg and breadcrumbs and fried.

## 'Mpanata

(Sicilia) Type of pizza with various toppings.

## 'Mpepata di cozze

(Campania) Mussels served in the cooking water with lemon, parsley.

## Mucca

Cow.

## Muccu

(Sicilia) Tiny sand smelt.

**Mucroncini**
(Piemonte) Dry sweet cakes.

**Muddica**
(Sicilia, Calabria) Breadcrumbs.

**Muddizzosu**
(Sardegna) Type of bread.

**Muffolette**
(Sicilia) Hot bread with oil and sesame seeds.

**Muflone**
(Sardegna) Wild sheep.

**Muggine**
(Emilia-Romagna) Grey mullet.

**Mugheddu**
(Sardegna) Salted, dried and smoked mullet.

**(Alla) Mugnaia**
'Miller's style'. Of fish, dipped in milk and flour, fried, with hot butter, lemon and parsley.

**Mulette**
(Molise) Pork sausage with hot pepper.

**Mulettu**
(Sicilia) Grey mullet.

**Mulis/mulze**
(Friuli-Venezia Giulia) Blood pudding with raisins, pine nuts, spices.

**Muller-Thurgau**
White grape variety, introduced from Germany, grown mainly in the northeast.

**Muntun a la sau**
(Piemonte) Spit-roasted mutton basted with oil, vinegar, hot pepper.

**(Alla) Muranese**
In the style of Murano island, *Veneto*. See *moleche*.

**Murena**
Moray eel.

**Murice**
Murex, small shellfish.

**Murseddu**
(Calabria) Flat bread filled with a spicy mixture of tripe, offal, tomatoes and hot pepper; also known as *morseddu, morzeddu*.

**Mursiellu alla catanzarese**
Rich pork and wine stew

**Mus**
(Trentino-Alto Adige) Sweet gruel of *polenta*, wheat flour and milk with poppy seeds; also known as *farinata alla contadina*.

**Musciam(me)e**
(Liguria) Dried dolphin, tuna or swordfish, eaten in thin slices with oil and garlic; also known as *mosciame, musseddu*.

**Muscoli**
Mussels.

**Muscolo/muscoletti**
Shank, of beef, veal.

**Muset**
(Friuli-Venezia Giulia) Spicy pork sausage, boiled and served with pickled turnips or *polenta*.

**Musillo**
Thick central cut of salt cod.

**Muso**
Muzzle, of beef.

**Musseddu**
See *musciame*.

**Mustazzoli**
See *mostaccioli*.

**Mustella**
Forkbeard, fish similar to whiting.

**Mùstica**
(Calabria) Tiny anchovies with hot pepper dried and preserved in oil.

## (Alla) Napoletana
In the style of Naples, *Campania*; interchangeable with *alla partenopea*. See *baccalà, braciolone, costolette, crostini, lasagna, olive, peperoni, perciatelli, pizza, ragù, ravioli, risotto, salame, sarde, spaghetti, stecchi, timballo, triglie, trippa, zite*.

## Nardi
Well-known producer of *grappa* and other spirits.

## Nasco
(Sardegna) White grape variety, producing sherry-type wines.

## Nasello
Whiting, hake. *N. alla marchigiana*: marinated and grilled, with anchovy and vinegar sauce. *N. alla palermitana*: baked with oil, herbs, anchovies.

## Natale
Christmas.

## Navone
Swede.

## 'Ncapriata
(Puglia) Dried beans stewed to a paste, with oil and other vegetables.

## 'Ndocca 'ndocca
(Abruzzo) Stewed pork offal, head, trotters, with peppers, vinegar and herbs.

## 'Ndugghia
(Calabria) Pork sausage, served with vegetable soup.

## Nebbiolo
Grape variety responsible for some of Italy's finest red wines, e.g. *Barolo* and *Barbaresco*.

## Necci
(Toscana, Emilia-Romagna) Sweet chestnut flour balls served with cheese.

## Negretti
Chocolate almond squares.

## Neonata
(Sicilia) Tiny sardines and anchovies.

## Negroamaro
(Puglia) Red grape variety, used in big rich wines.

## Nepitelle
(Calabria) Sweet cheese pastries; also known as *pitte nepite*.

## Nero
Black.

## Nervetti/nervitt

(Lombardia) Salad of boiled calf's feet cut into thin strips, with onions.

## Nespola

Loquat, Japanese medlar, the fruit.

## (Di) Nicosia

Of Nicosia, *Sicilia*. See *salsiccia*.

## (Al) Nido

'In a nest', one ingredient in another.

## Nirvi e musse

(Molise) Salad of calf's muzzle.

## Niuleddas de meli

(Sardegna) Sweetmeats of candied orange, nuts, spices etc.

## Nocchetedde

(Calabria) Pasta bows, served with cheese and a sauce.

## Nocciole

Hazelnuts. *N.'ndrite* (Campania): roasted.
Noisettes, boned chops.

## Nocciolini

(Piemonte, Lombardia) Tiny macaroons, sometimes with hazelnuts.

## Noce

Nut. Walnut. *Noce di cocco*: coconut. *Noce moscata*: nutmeg.
Rump, of meat. Knob, of butter.

## Nociata

(Lazio) Honey and walnut nougat.

## Nocino

(Emilia-Romagna) Liqueur of green walnuts steeped in spirit.

## Nodino
Chop, of meat.

## (Alla) Nonna
'Grandmother's style'. Often used to indicate some homely preparation.

## Nonnati
Goby, tiny sea fish.

## (Alla) Norcina
In the style of Norcia, *Umbria*. With truffles. With sausage, onion, cream and truffle sauce, of pasta. See also *beccaccia, cosciotto*.

## Norma
See *spaghetti*.

## Normanno
(Sicilia) Popular red and white wines made by Diego, Rallo.

## Noto
(Sicilia) *DOC* wines made from the *Moscato* grape.

## (Alla) Novarese
In the style of Novara, *Piemonte*. See *anitra, minestrone, pomodori, risotto*.

## Noxe
See *salsa*.

## Nuragus
(Sardegna) White grape variety.

## 'Nzuddi
(Calabria) Honey sweetmeats in various shapes.

## Oca

Goose. *O. farcita alla borghese*: stuffed with pork, apples, chestnuts and the liver, roast. *O. di guerra* (Piemonte): pieces poached in water, cooled in own fat.

## Oca Goose.

*O. farcita alla borghese*: stuffed with pork, apples, chestnuts and the liver, roast. *O. di guerra* (Piemonte): pieces poached in water, cooled in own fat.

## Occhialone/occhiata

Sea bream.

## Occhi di lupo

Short pasta tubes.

## Occhione/occhi verdi

Deep-water sea fish with green eyes.

## Offelle

(Lombardia) Sweet oval pastries.
(Friuli-Venezia Giulia) Pasta squares filled with veal, sausage, spinach.

## (All') Olandese

Dutch style. With hollandaise sauce *(salsa olandese)*.

## Olevano Romano

(Lazio) Red *DOC* wine from *Cesanese* grapes.

## Oliena

(Sardegna) Village and wine made by local cooperative.

## Olio

Oil. *Sott' olio*: preserved in oil, of vegetables, fish.

## Olive

Olives. *O. all' anconetana/all' ascolana*: giant green olives stuffed with meat, ham or chicken, deep fried. *O. nere alla napoletana*: black olives marinated in oil, lemon, herbs. *O. verde alla siciliana*: green olives stuffed with puréed tomatoes, peppers and capers.

## Olivette

'Olives', of beef, veal. *O. di vitello alla pesarese*: veal rolls stuffed with ham, cooked in wine and tomato sauce.

## (All') Olivitana

See *trippa*.

## Oltrepò Pavese

(Lombardia) Prolific wine-growing region, with 10 *DOC*s, 6 named according to grape variety; many fine wines are produced outside the regulations and sold under estate labels.

## Ombrina

Umbrine, similar to large sea bass.

## Omeletta

French-style omelette.

## Orata

Gilt-head sea bream. *O. alla barese*: marinated with oil and herbs, charcoal grilled. *O. alla partenopea*: poached with wine, herbs and tomato sauce. *O. alla pugliese*: baked with potatoes, cheese and parsley.

## Orecchio

Ear, e.g. of pig.
*Orecchia marina*: ormer, abalone, small ear-shaped shellfish.

## Orecchiette

(Puglia) Homemade pasta in the form of small shells, served with rich meat sauce or with broccoli and anchovies.

## Origano

Oregano.

## Oristano

(Sardegna) White *DOC* wine similar to sherry, based on *Vernaccia* grapes.

## O'rraù

See *ragù*.

## Ortaggi

Vegetables, greens.

## Ortiche

Nettles.

## Orvieto

(Umbria) Town famous for *DOC* white wine, mainly from *Trebbiano*; traditionally semi-sweet, now usually dry.

## Orzo

Barley. *O. perlato*: pearl barley.
Tiny pasta grains, for soup.

## Osei/oseleti

See *polenta*.

## Ossibuchi/ossobuchi/osso buco/oss buss

(Lombardia) Braised shin of veal, finished with lemon peel, garlic and herbs and served with rice.

## (All') Ossolana

In the style of Domodossola, *Piemonte*. See *gnocchi, lumache*.

## Osteria

Hostelry, inn.

## Ostia

Wafer.

## Ostriche

Oysters. *O. alla tarantina*: baked with oil and parsley. *O. alla veneziana*: grilled with oil and herbs.

## Ostuni

(Puglia) Town producing red and white *DOC* wines, the red from *Ottavianello* grapes.

## Ottarde

Bustard, bird.

## Ottavianello

Red grape variety grown in the south.

## Ovada

(Piemonte) Light red *DOC* wine from *Dolcetto* grapes.

## Ovini

Sheep.

## Ovoli/ovuli

See *funghi*.

## Ovotàrica

See *bottarga*.

**Padella**
Frying pan.

**Padellete**
(Emilia-Romagna) Baked pork ribs with beans.

**(Alla) Padovana**
In the style of Padua, *Veneto*. See *pollo, risotto.*

**(Alla) Paesana**
'Country style'. With bacon, mushrooms, perhaps tomatoes, especially of pasta.

**Paeta al malgaragno**
(Veneto) Roast turkey with pomegranate sauce.

**Pagello**
Sea bream.

**Paglia e fieno**
Mixed yellow and green thin pasta noodles (resembling 'straw and hay'). *P.e.f. alla ghiotta*: with cream, ham and mushroom sauce.

**Paglierino/pagliarini**
(Piemonte) Type of cheese.

**Pagnotta**
Loaf, of bread.
*P. Santa Chiara* (Campania): potato bread filled with tomatoes, anchovies and herbs.

**Pagro**
Sea bream.

**Paillard**
Veal steak beaten thin and grilled.

**Pajata**
(Lazio) Sucking calf innards cooked with herbs, white wine, hot pepper and tomato, baked with potatoes or served with pasta.

**Palamita**
Bonito, fish like small tuna.

**(Alla) Palermitana**
In the style of Palermo, *Sicilia*. See *caponata, carciofi, ficato, nasello, sarde, spaghetti.*

**Palle di neve**
Sugar-coated nut balls.

**Pallini**
Ball-shaped sweets.

## Palombacce

Wood pigeon. *P. alla ghiotta* (Umbria): spit-roasted, basted with a sauce of wine, ham, liver and capers. *P. alla perugina*: spit-roasted, with a sauce of red wine, the entrails, juniper berries, olives. *P. alla todina*: finished in a pan with red wine, ham and the entrails.

## Palombo

Ring dove.
Shark.

## Pampàvia

(Piemonte) Small biscuits.

## Pampepato

(Emilia-Romagna, Marche) Ring-shaped nut cake, with pepper and sometimes grape must.

## Pan

Bread, cake. *P. dolce* (Liguria): yeast bread with sultanas, pine nuts, candied citron. *P. de frizze* (Friuli): loaf with pork scratchings. *P. de mei* (Lombardia): round sweet yeast bun. *P. d'oro* (Veneto): light yeast cake. *P. di Spagna*: sponge cake. *P. ed Nadell/speziale* (Emilia-Romagna): spicy Christmas cake with nuts, candied fruit, chocolate. *P. zal* (Friuli-Venezia Giulia): maize flour cake.

## Panada

(Veneto) Broth thickened with breadcrumbs, eggs, parmesan.

## Panafracchi

See *ciambelle*.

## Panarda

(Abruzzo) Feast of 20 or more dishes traditional at celebrations and holidays, occasionally staged by restaurants.

## Pancetta

Unsmoked belly bacon, cured in salt and spices and rolled up in a sausage.

## Pancotto

(Lazio, Puglia, Calabria) Bread soup, sometimes with seasonal vegetables, potatoes, herbs, finished with oil and cheese; also known as *pappa*.

## Pandolce/pandoro

See *pan*.

## Pandorato

(Lazio) Slices of bread with *mozzarella* cheese and anchovies, dipped in milk and egg and fried.

## Pane

Bread. *P. a birra* (Sicilia): loaf sprinkled with sesame seeds; *p. forte* is similar. *P. carasau* (Sardegna): paper thin crisp bread; also known as *carta/fogli di musica, fresa, pistocco*. *P. frattau*: the same softened in hot

broth, served with tomatoes, cheese and eggs; also known as *panifrattau*. *P. di San Siro* (Lombardia): rich chocolate and nut cake, named for the patron saint of Pavia.

**Panelle**
(Sardegna) Chick pea flour fritters.

**Panettone**
(Lombardia) Spiced yeast cake with sultanas and candied fruit.

**Panforte**
(Toscana) Rich spicy cake with candied fruit and nuts.

**Pangiallo familiare di Natale**
(Lazio) Spicy cake with raisins and nuts.

**Pangrattato**
Breadcrumbs.

**Paniccia**
See *panissa*.

**Panifrattau**
See *pane*.

**Panino**
Bread roll. *P. al ramerino* (Toscana): with oil, sultanas and herbs.

**Paniscia**
(Piemonte) Rice cooked in bean and sausage broth.

**Panissa**
(Liguria) Boiled chick pea flour and onions, usually sliced and fried.

## Panna
Cream. *P. cotta*: cream with burnt sugar, type of crême caramel; or coffee-flavoured cream custard. *P. montata*: whipped cream, usually heavily sweetened.

## Pannerone
Version of *stracchino* cheese.

## Pannocchie
Mantis shrimp.

## Pansot(t)i
(Liguria) Triangular pasta envelopes stuffed with spinach, chard, *ricotta* cheese, perhaps brains, sweetbreads, traditionally served with walnut sauce.

## Pantelleria
(Sicilia) Island with *DOC* for sweet wines of varying strengths made from local variety of *Moscato*.

## Panunto
(Tuscany) Local name for garlic toast *(bruschetta)*.

## Panspeziale
(Emilia-Romagna) Honey cake with aniseed, raisins, nuts and chocolate.

## Panzanella
(Lazio, Toscana, Campania) Bread and tomato salad with anchovies, onions, oil, herbs.

## Panzarotti/panzerotti
(Campania, Basilicata, Puglia) Deep fried or baked pastries with a filling, usually of ham and cheese, sometimes sweet. See also *calzone*.

## (Alla) Papalina
'Pope's style' (Lazio). With ham, eggs, cream plus parmesan, of pasta.
*Papaline*: sprats, small fish.

## Paparot
(Friuli-Venezia Giulia) Spinach and *polenta* soup.

## (Al) Papavero
With poppy seeds.

## Papazoi
(Friuli-Venezia Giulia) Bean, barley and sweetcorn soup.

## Pappa al pomodoro
(Toscana) Tomatoes cooked with oil, garlic and basil. See also *pancotto*.

## Pappardelle
Long strips of pasta, often with a crimped edge. *P. del Cantunzein*: mixed yellow and green noodles with peppers, tomatoes and sausage; after the Bologna restaurant famous for pasta. *P. alla/sulla lepre* (Toscana): with rich hare stew.

## Paprica (dolce)
Paprika.

## Paradiso
See *torta*.

## Paragho
(Toscana) Sea bream.

## Pardulas
(Sardegna) Small pastry rolls stuffed with cheese and sprinkled with honey.

## Parigina
(Sicilia) Traditional bread.

## (Alla) Parmigiana
In the style of Parma, *Emilia-Romagna*. With parmesan cheese. See also *coniglio, prosciutto, risotto*.
*Parmigiana (di melanzane)* (Campania, Sicilia, Basilicata, Calabria, Puglia): aubergines baked with parmesan, *mozzarella* cheese and tomato sauce, and sometimes further ingredients; also applied to courgettes, cardoons.

## Parmigiano-Reggiano
(Emilia-Romagna, Lombardia) Parmesan cheese, hard, finely grained, straw coloured and fruity, with the name etched on a brown crust; made by traditional methods within a defined area and aged for at least 18 months, called *vecchio* when 2 years old, *stravecchio* at 3, *stravecchione* at 4.

**(La) Parrina**
(Toscana) Popular red and white *DOC* wines.

**Parrozzo**
(Abruzzo) Round almond cake covered in chocolate.

**(Alla) Partenopea**
(Campania) Neapolitan style; from the Siren Parthenope associated with the city. See *cannelloni, cervella, orata, peperoni, saltimbocca, torta, uova.*

**Pasquale/pasqualino**
Of Easter.

**Passacrassana**
Variety of pear.

**Passato**
Strained. Mashed, puréed. *P. al burro*: sautéed in butter. *P. ai ferri*: grilled. *P. al forno*: baked.

**Passatelli**
(Romagna, Marche) Strands of parmesan, egg and breadcrumbs, with meat sometimes added, in broth.

**Passera**
Plaice, flat sea fish.

**Passito**
Wine made from semi-dried grapes, usually very sweet.

**Passoliate**
(Puglia) Dry almond and raisin cake.

## Pasta

Pasta, i.e. paste or dough of flour, water and perhaps eggs, formed into an infinite variety of shapes and sizes, including the familiar macaroni, spaghetti and lasagne, or sometimes incorporating a stuffing, like ravioli, or coloured green with spinach; available dried as a commercial product, or freshly made. The traditional first course of southern Italy, eaten plainly boiled, with a sauce *(p. asciutta)*, in soup *(p. in brodo)*, or finished in the oven as a composite dish. *P. ammiscata* (Campania): miscellaneous pasta bits in bean soup. *P. cunscia* (Lombardia): pasta of various shapes boiled with potatoes, plus tomato sauce. *P. fritta* (Campania): rich omelette with pasta, meat sauce, ham and cheese. *P. con il riquagghiu* (Sicilia): spaghetti or short macaroni mixed with beaten egg and cheese.

Pastry. *P. frolla*: shortcrust. *P. sfoglia*: puff.

Cake. *P. genovese*: lemon sponge cake.

Paste, e.g. of anchovies.

*Pastella*: batter for frying.

## Pastecresciute

(Campania) Savoury fritters.

## Pasticceria

Pastries, cakes, confectionery. Pastrycook's, confectioner's shop.

## Pasticcini

Biscuits, pastries, small cakes.

## Pasticcio

Baked pie or composition, of meat, pasta, or vegetables and cheese etc. *P. di maccheroncelli alla fiorentina*: beef, mushrooms, chicken livers, pasta tubes and tomatoes in pastry. *P. pesarese*: beef stew with herbs and spices, red wine, tomatoes. See also *cappello da gendarme.*

Pâté, loaf, cold mould, of meat, fish.

*Pasticciato*: baked, made into a pie. See also *polenta.*

## Pastiera

(Campania) Elaborate pastry of *ricotta* cheese, candied fruit, spices.

## Pastina/pastine

Tiny pasta shapes, for soups.

## Pastinache

Parsnips.

## Pastissada/pastizzada

(Veneto, Friuli-Venetia Giulia) Beef or horse stew with vinegar, wine, spices, served with dumplings or *polenta;* also known as *ciâr pastizzade.* See also *polenta.*

## (Alla) Pastora

'Shepherd's-style'. See *maccheroni.*

## Pastorella

Small version of *bel paese* cheese.

## (Del) Pasubio
Of the Pasubio valleys, *Veneto*. See *soppressa*.

## Patate
Potatoes. *P. alla borghese*: with butter and lemon. *P. sabbiose*: saute potatoes. *P. alla triestina*: fried with onions. *P. alla veneziana*: fried cubes with onions and herbs.

## Patedda
(Sardegna) Mixed boiled meats – boar, goat, lamb – with vegetables and cheese; also known as *pingiada*.

## Patelle
Limpets, small shellfish.

## Paternostri
(Calabria) Pasta cubes, served with cheese and a sauce.

## (Alla) Pavese
In the style of Pavia, *Lombardia*. See *zuppa*.
Large hard bread loaf; also known as *miccone*.

## Pazlache
See *agnolotti*.

## Pearà
(Veneto) Beef marrow, cheese and pepper sauce, served hot with cold boiled meat.

## Pecc ed vaca
(Piemonte) Boiled pressed cow's udder, served sliced as a first course.

## Pecora
Sheep, ewe.

## Pecorelle
(Basilicata) Snails in tomato and herb sauce.

## Pecorino
(Lazio, Toscana, Abruzzo, Sardegna, Sicilia) Cheese originally of sheep's milk, either soft and mild, or more usually dry, sharp and salty; made especially around Rome – *P. romano*, also known as *romano*; with other regional versions – *p. sardo*, also known as *formaggio fiore, fiore sardo* and *sardo*; and *p. siciliano*, also known as *canestrato*.

## Pelato
Peeled, skinned.

## Pellaro
(Calabria) Robust red non-*DOC* wine.

## Penne/pennini/pennoni
Short quill-shaped tubes of pasta, either ridged or smooth.

## Peoci
(Veneto) Mussels.

## Pepatelli
(Abruzzo) Peppery honey and almond biscuits.

## Pepe
Pepper. *P. di caienna*: cayenne pepper.

## Peperata
See *peverada*.

## Peperonata
Sweet pepper and tomato stew.

## Peperoncino (rosso)
Hot red pepper, chili pepper.

## Peperoni
Sweet peppers, pimientos. *P. alla calabrese*: stewed with tomatoes. *P. imbottiti alla barese/alla napoletana*: stuffed with olives, capers, anchovies, baked. *P. gratinati alla partenopea*: baked with capers, olives, anchovies, pine nuts. *P. alla piemontese*: baked, stuffed with garlic, tomato and anchovy, served cold. *P. in padella alla romana*: fried with onions and tomatoes.

## Peposo
(Toscana) Shin of beef stewed with tomatoes, wine, pepper.

## Perchia
Sea perch, comber.

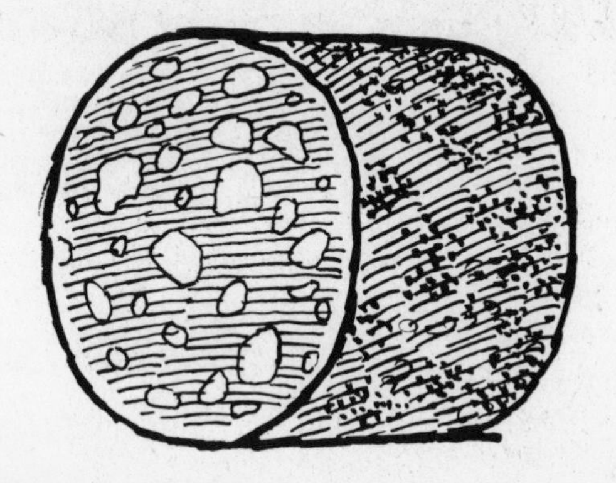

## Perciatell(on)i

(Campania, Calabria) Long hollow pasta noodles. *P. principi di Napoli*: with chicken breast, peas, cheese and a sauce from braised beef.

## Perda Rubia

(Sardegna) Branded wine made from *Cannonau* grapes by Mario Mereu.

## Pere

Pears. *P. ripiene* (Lombardia): stuffed with *gorgonzola* cheese. *Pera martina/martin sec*: small firm cooking variety.

## Per'e Palummo

(Campania) 'Dove's foot'. Red grape variety; also known as *Piedirosso*.

## Pernice

Partridge. *P. alla sarda*: boiled or simply marinated and preserved in oil. *P. alla siciliana*: stewed in oil and wine with olives.

*Pernicette*: tiny pasta rings, for soup.

## Persicata

(Lombardia) Peach paste, dried and cut into squares.

## Persico

River perch.

*Persico-trota*: black bass.

## (Alla) Perugina

In the style of Perugia, *Umbria*. See *cardi, colombo, crostata, gobbi, lonza, palombacce, pizza, scaloppine*.

## (Alla) Pesarese

In the style of Pesaro, *Marche*. See *coniglio, olivette, pasticcio, seppie*.

## (Alla) Pescatora

'Fisherman's style'. See *roscioli*.

## Pescatrice

See *rane*.

## Pesce

Fish. *P. balestra*: trigger fish.

*P. cappone*: rascasse, scorpion fish.

*P. castagna*: sea bream, pomfret.

*P. forca*: gurnard.

*P. gatto*: dogfish.

*P.lucertola*: lizard fish.

*P.martello*: hammerhead shark.

*P. persico*: river perch. *P. p. all'umbra*: poached, with butter, lemon, parsley.

*P. pilota*: pilot fish.

*P. prete*: star-gazer, fish with upturned eyes (like a 'priest').

*P. San Pietro*: John Dory; also known as *p. gallo* in *Sicilia*.

*P. sciabola*: scabbard fish; also known as *p. argentin* in *Liguria*.

*P. serra*: blue fish.

*P. spada*: swordfish.

*P. specchie*: bony red fish, used in soup.

*P. stocco* (Calabria, Sicilia): dried cod.

*P. da taglio*: halibut.

*P. turchino*: mackerel.

*P. violino*: guitar fish.

*P.volante*: flying fish.

## Pescecane

Dogfish, shark.

## Pescestocco

(Sicilia) Dried cod. *P. alla messinese*: stewed in oil with onions, tomatoes, potatoes, capers etc.

## Pesche

Peaches. *P. ripiene/alla genovese/alla piemontese*: stuffed with macaroon and finished in the oven.

*Pesche noce*: nectarines.

## Pesta

(Friuli-Venezia Giulia) Finely chopped salt pork, added to soup.

## Pesto

(Liguria) Basil sauce with garlic, cheese and oil, sometimes pine nuts, served especially with pasta and soup.

## Pestun de fave

See *marò*.

## Petit Rouge

(Valle d'Aosta) Red grape variety.

## Petrale

(Liguria) Flat sea fish.

## (Alla) Petroniana

See *fegatelli*.

### Pettine
Small scallops, shellfish.

### Pettirossi
Robins.

### Petto
Breast, e.g. of veal. *Petti di pollo*: filleted chicken breasts. *P. di p. alla fiorentina*: fried in butter. *P. di p. alla senese*: sautéed, with lemon and parsley.

### Pèttole
(Puglia, Basilicata) Small sweet fritters.

### Peverada
(Veneto) Peppery sauce served with roast meat; also known as *peperata*. See also *riso*.

### (Alla) Piacentina
In the style of Piacenza, *Emilia-Romagna*. See *capretto*.

### (A) Piacere
To your pleasure, to your taste.

### Piacintinu
(Sicilia) Version of *pecorino* cheese with pepper and saffron.

### Piad(in)a (romagnola)
Rustic flat bread, usually served warm with ham or sausage and cheese; also known as *piè*.

### Piatto
Plate. *Al piatto*: shirred, gently cooked in a dish, of eggs. *Fra i due piatti*: between 2 plates, steamed, of fish, beef or veal.

Dish, course, of a meal. *Piatto del giorno*: dish of the day.

*Piatto elefante* (Trentino-Alto Adige): feast of appetizers, followed by a variety of meats with rice, a range of vegetables, finally cheese, fruit and cakes; a speciality of the Elefante restaurant, Bressanone.

### Piave
(Veneto) *DOC* wine area with 4 authorized types, named according to grape variety.

### Piccage
(Liguria) Pasta ribbons, usually served with *pesto* or artichoke sauce.

### Piccante
Piquant, spicy. With a pepper sauce.

### Piccata
Very thin veal escalopes, often served sautéed, with lemon juice.

### (A) Picchipacchio
See *chiocciole*.

## Piccione/piccioncello/piccioncino

Pigeon, squab. *P. alla spoletina*: with black olives.

## Piccolo

Small.

## Picellati

(Molise) Pastries filled with honey, nuts, grape must.

## Pici

(Toscana) Homemade pasta noodles, served with cheese.

## Picolit

White grape variety, native of *Friuli*. Its wines were once compared with those of Château d'Yquem and considered amongst the greatest dessert wines of Europe; now very rare.

## Picula 'd caval

(Emilia-Romagna) Stewed horsemeat with oil and tomatoes.

## Pie

Foot. *Pie d'asino*: dog cockle, small shellfish. *P. di pelicano*: small cone-shaped shellfish. See also *piadina*.

## Piedini

Feet, trotters, e.g. of pig. See also *batsoà*.

## Piedirosso

See *Per'e Palummo*.

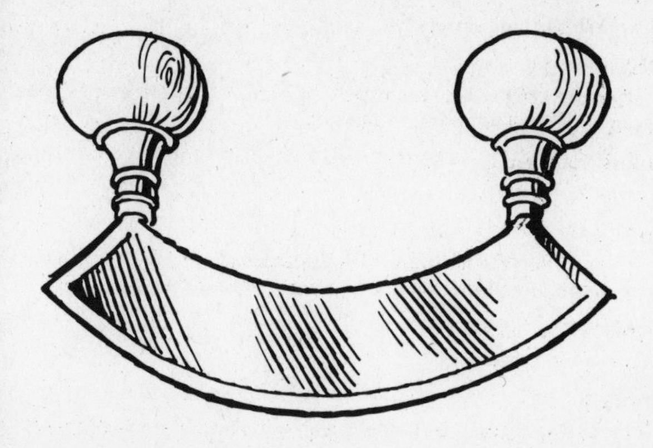

**(Alla) Piemontese**
In the style of *Piemonte*. With meat and truffle sauce, of pasta. With *fontina* cheese and truffles, of veal escalopes, turkey breasts. See also *batsoà, cavolfiore, gnocchi, lumache, manzo, peperoni, pesche, quadretti, risotto, spezzatino, spinaci, tartuffi, timballo, uova.*

**Pieno**
Full, complete. Full-bodied.

**Pigato**
(Liguria) White grape variety.

**Piglio**
(Lazio) Small town known for red *DOC* wine from *Cesanese* grapes; may be dry or sweet and sometimes sparkling.

**Pigna di Pasqua**
See *casatiello*.

**Pignat(t)a**
Cooking pot, often earthenware. (Basilicata) Lamb stew with vegetables and cheese simmered lengthily in such a pot. See also *minestra*.

**Pignoli**
Pine nuts, pine kernels.

**Pignolata**
(Sicilia) Cone-shaped confection of sugar- and chocolate-coated cakes.

**Pignuetti**
(Liguria) Mixed fried fish.

**Pillas/pillus**
(Sardegna) Pasta sheets layered with meat, ham, cheese, hard-boiled eggs and tomato sauce, finished in the oven.

**Pilau**
(Sardegna) Pilaff rice, usually with kid or lamb.

**(Alla) Pilota**
See *pesce, risotto*.

**Pimpinella**
Pimpernelle, wild salad green

**Pinaroli**
Small fungi found in pine woods.

**Pincinelle**
(Marche) Long thin pasta strands. *P. all'anconetana*: served with meat sauce and cheese.

**Pincisgrassi**
See *vincisgrassi*.

**Pingiada**
See *patedda*.

**Pinne**
Fan mussels.

**Pinoccate**
(Umbria) Almond and pine nut cakes.

**Pinoli**
Pine nuts.

**Pinot**
Family of grape varieties, native of Burgundy, grown in the north; often known by German names. *P. bianco*: white Pinot; also known as *Weissburgunder*. *P. Chardonnay*: most important white grape of Burgundy; not strictly a Pinot. *P. grigio*: Pinot Gris, Tokay from Alsace; known as *Ruländer*. *P. nero*: Pinot Noir of Burgundy; also known as *Blauburgunder*.

**Pinza**
(Trentino-Alto Adige, Veneto, Friuli-Venezia Giulia) Dried fig cake.

**Pinzimonio**
Dip of olive oil, salt and pepper, for raw vegetables.

**Pipitone**
(Calabria) Eel.

**Pirciatu**
(Sicilia) Long hollow pasta noodles.

## (Alla) Pisana
In the style of Pisa, *Toscana*. See *cedioli*.

## Pisano di San Torpé
(Toscana) Dry white wine *(DOC)* based on *Trebbiano* grapes.

## Pisarei e fasö
(Emilia-Romagna) Tiny bread dumplings with tomato sauce and beans.

## Pisci
(Sicilia) Fish. See also *pesce*.
*Pisci d'ovu*: fritters of egg batter (fried like tiny fish).
*Piscistoccu*: dried cod.

## Piselli
Peas. *P. all' antica*: cooked with lettuce and finished with cream. *P. alla borghese*: with onion, ham and herbs.
*Pisellata*: dish of peas. *P. alla maceratese*: with bacon, garlic, tomatoes.
*Pisellini (dolce)*: Tiny early peas, petit pois. *P. alla fiorentina*: stewed with ham.

## Pissaladeira
See *sardenaira*.

## Pistacchi
Pistachio nuts.

## Pistocco
See *pane*.

## Pistum
(Friuli-Venezia Giulia) Sweet bread dumplings with raisins in pork broth.

## (Con) Pitaggio
See *polpette*.

## Pitigliano
(Toscana) Dry white *DOC* wine from Trebbiano grapes.

## Pitò
(Piemonte) Turkey. *P. al fieno maggengo*: boiled with hay.

## Pitta
(Calabria) Flat bread, pizza, with a variety of toppings. *P. chicculiata/picchiulata:* with tomatoes and hot pepper. *P. maniata*: sandwiched with eggs, cheese, sausage, hot pepper. *P. 'nchiusa*: sweet, enclosing nuts, raisins, grape must. See also *nepitelle*.

## Pittedre
(Puglia) Fruit pastries.

## Pizza

(Campania) Round of yeast dough spread with tomatoes, *mozzarella* cheese, anchovies and herbs, baked in a brick oven – the classic *pizza alla napoletana*, as sold in the pizzerias of Naples. *P. Margherita*: with tomatoes, *mozzarella* and parmesan; after an Italian queen. *P. alla marinara*: with tomatoes and garlic, the traditional homemade version. *P. alla romana*: with onions, or with anchovies, *mozzarella* and parmesan.

Pie, pizza-type preparation, often with yeast pastry. *P. alla catanese*: sandwiched with veal, anchovies, cheese, olives. *P. alla cagliaritana*: potato pastry topped with tomatoes, anchovies, cheese. *P. alla perugina*: enclosing ham and cheese; also known as *p. al testo*: without ham. *P. rustica* (Abruzzo, Puglia): sweet pastry case filled with ham, sausage, cheese and eggs. See also *cuddiruni, sardenaira, sfuicione*.

Sweet tart, cake. *P. dolce* (Abruzzo): sponge cake soaked in liqueur, layered with chocolate and almond cream, glazed with sugar. *P. di Pasqua* (Marche): sweet yeast cake; also known as *torta di Pasqua*. *P. pasquale* (Lazio): cheese and honey cake. See also *castagnaccio*.

## (Alla) Pizzaiola

(Campania) With tomato, garlic and herb sauce. With anchovies and *mozzarella* cheese. With tomatoes and capers.

## Pizzella

Pizza pie with a filling, pizza round. *Pizzelle alla barese*: potato pastries topped with tomato and cheese. *P. casalinghe* (Campania): fried pastries filled with escarole, capers, anchovies, olives, sultanas.

## Pizzeria

Simple restaurant, serving quick cheap meals prepared before the customers, often in wood-burning oven.

## Pizzette

Miniature pizzas.

## Pizzicotti
(Calabria) Tiny pasta cylinders, for soup.

## Pizzoccheri
(Lombardia) Short broad pasta noodles made of buckwheat flour, usually boiled with potatoes, chard etc. and served with cheese.

## Pocio
See *bigoli*.

## Polcevera
(Liguria) Light, dry white wine.

## Polenta
(Lombardia, Veneto) Yellow maize flour, corn meal, boiled and eaten hot with butter and cheese, alone or as an accompaniment to meat, or cooled, sliced and fried, grilled or finished in the oven. *P. alla bergamasca*: baked, with tomatoes, sausage, cheese. *P. al forno alla bolzanese*: similar, with sausage and bacon. *P. concia/cunsa/valdostana*: with cheese, either boiled or finished in oven. *P. condita* (Friuli-Venezia Giulia): fried, with bacon and sage. *P. cunscia* (Lombardia): boiled, 'enriched' with butter and garlic. *P. al frumentino* (Piemonte): of buckwheat flour, baked with anchovies, cheese. *P. grassa* (Piemonte): boiled, with cheese, butter, perhaps sausages. *P. alla lodigiana*: rounds sandwiched with cheese, egg-and-breadcrumbed and fried. *P. e osei* (Veneto, Lombardia): with small birds, spit-roasted and in sauce. *P. con oseleti scampai* (Veneto): fried slices topped with skewered meats and mushrooms. *P. pasticciata* (Lombardia): slices layered with meat sauce, butter, cheese and finished in oven; with many variations, e.g. the addition of béchamel and mushrooms, or tomato and sausage (*alla ciociara/romagnola*), or truffles (*de siouri*), or chicken giblets (*pastizzada alla veneta*). *P. rustida* (Lombardia): fried slices, with onion, milk, cheese. *P. alla sarda*: with tomato, cheese and sausage. *P. taragna* (Lombardia): of buckwheat and maize flour, stirred with the 'tarello', plus butter, cheese.

(*Alla) polenta*: prepared like *polenta*, of e.g. beans.

Sweet dish involving or resembling *polenta*. *P. d'Ivrea*: buckwheat flour cake flavoured with vanilla. *P. dolce* (Lombardia): maize cake with macaroons and cinnamon. *P. e osei* (Lombardia): sponge cake layered with apricot jam and decorated with chocolate birds.

## (Alla) Polesana
In the style of Polesine, *Veneto*. See *risotto*.

## Polip(ett)o
Octopus; or small squid.

## Poliporo
Fungus which grows on trees.

## Pollame
Poultry.

## Pollastra/pollastr(ell)o
Pullet, cockerel, young chicken.

## Pollino
(Calabria) *DOC* zone for red wine based on *Gaglioppo* grapes.

## Pollo
Chicken. *P. grillettato all'aretina*: cooked with wine and onions, served with rice. *P. alla babi* (Piemonte): spit-roast over charcoal. *P. alla cacciatora*: sautéed with green peppers and tomatoes. *P. fritto alla fiorentina*: battered, and fried, with lemon. *P. alla Franceschiello* (Abruzzo): spit-roasted with olives and pickles; after Frances II, king of Naples. *P. in intingolo alla friulana*: simmered in wine, with sausage, mushrooms and giblets. *P. alla padovana*: in fricassee, finished with egg yolks and lemon. *P. alla romana*: stewed with white wine, tomato, ham and herbs, plus peppers. *P. ripieno alla trentina*: stuffed with nuts, bread, beef marrow, liver and boiled.

## Polmone
Lung, of veal.

## Polpa
Meat, flesh.

## Polpessa/polpetiello
Octopus.

## Polpett(a)e
Meat balls. *P. di maiale con pitaggio* (Sicilia): fried pork and cheese balls, with artichokes, peas, beans. Croquettes, of vegetables. See also *melanzane*.

## Polpettone
Loaf, sausage, of meat , poultry, fish. *P. alla toscana*: meat and cheese loaf, braised in wine with tomatoes, or fried, or poached in broth.

Cake, baked mixture, of vegetables. *P. alla genovese*: potatoes and French beans with cheese and eggs.

## Polpo (di scoglio)
Octopus. *P. abruzzese in purgatorio*: stewed in oil with tomatoes, garlic, hot pepper. *P. alla Luciana*: very similar; or poached in water, served with oil and lemon.

## Pomino
Village in the Rufina district of *Chianti* with own *DOC* for red and white wines.

## Pommarola
(Campania) Tomato sauce, for pasta.

## Pomodori
Tomatoes. *P. ripieni alla novarese*: stuffed with rice, onion, cheese, egg-and-breadcrumbed and deep fried. *P. sott'olio* (Puglia, Calabria): dried in the sun and preserved in oil with various herbs and spices. *P. di magro alla sarda*: stuffed with anchovy, tuna and aubergine, baked.

## Porceddu/porcetto
(Sardegna) Spit-roasted sucking pig with myrtle and other herbs.

## Porchetta
(Umbria, Marche, Lazio) Spit-roasted sucking pig, with fennel, rosemary, garlic etc.

*(Alla/In) porchetta*: prepared with the same herbs, of duck, rabbit, ham, carp, shellfish.

## Porcini
See *funghi*.

## Porpore
Murex, small shellfish.

## Porri
Leeks.

## Posciandra
See *bottagio*.

## Potabile
Drinking, drinkable, of water.

## (A/In) Potacchio
(Marche) Stewed with tomato, hot pepper, herbs and white wine, of lamb, poultry, dried cod.

## Potizza
(Friuli-Venezia Giulia) Yeast pastry with nuts, raisins, chocolate; also known as *presnitz*, *putizza*.

## Poveracce
(Emilia-Romagna) Small clams.

## (Alla) Poverella/(del) povero
'Poor man's style'. See *zuppa*.

## Powidl
(Friuli-Venezia Giulia) Prunes.

**Praio**
Sea bream.

**Pramaggiore**
(Veneto) Small town with *DOC* for red wines based on *Cabernet* and *Merlot* grapes.

**Pratai(u)olo**
Of the meadows.
*Prataioli*: field mushrooms.

**(Alla) Pratese**
In the style of Prato, *Toscana*. See *sedano*.

**Preboggion**
(Liguria) Mixture of wild greens and herbs – beet, borage etc. – as a stuffing for pasta, or soup.

**Prescinseua/prescinsöe**
(Liguria) Curd cheese.

**Presnitz**
See *potizza*.

**Prete**
See *cappello, pesce*.

**Prezzemolo**
Parsley.

**Primavera/primaverile**
Spring. With fresh spring vegetables.

**Primitivo**
(Puglia) Red grape variety (the name refers to its early ripening).

## Primizie
First, early, vegetables.

## Primo
First. *Primi*: first course of a meal – pasta, rice, etc. or soup.
*Primo sale* (Sicilia): cheese.

## Probusti
(Trentino-Alto Adige) Small smoked pork and veal sausages, eaten boiled with sauerkraut.

## Produttore
Producer, especially of wine.

## Profumato (al)
Flavoured (with).

## Prosciutto
Ham, usually salted and air-cured, often eaten raw rather than cooked. *P. di montagna*: raw country ham. *P. di Parma*: the famous Parma ham, lightly salted and dried, eaten raw in thin slices with figs, melon or butter. *P. del Montefeltro*: salted, with vinegar and pepper. *P. di San Daniele*: similar to Parma ham, produced on a small scale.

## Prosecco
(Veneto) White grape variety.

## Provatura
(Lazio) Mild cheese similar to *mozzarella*, originally of buffalo's milk, now rare and replaced by *provolone*.

## Provola
(Campania) Smooth bland cheese of buffalo's or sheep's milk, similar to *mozzarella*, fresh or smoked.

## Provolone
(Campania, Lombardia) Smooth supple fat cheese, mild to strong depending on age, occasionally still made from buffalo's milk and similar to *mozzarella*; moulded by hand in many different shapes, usually round or oval.

## Prugne (secche)
Prunes.

**Prugnuoli**
St George's mushrooms.

**Puccia**
(Piemonte) Pork and vegetables mixed with *polenta*, sometimes cooled, sliced and fried.

**(Alla) Puccini**
See *folaghe*.

**Puddica**
(Puglia) Pizza pie filled with tomatoes, olives, anchovies.

**Puddighinos a pienu**
(Sardegna) Small chickens stuffed with the giblets, tomatoes, eggs, and baked.

**(Alla) Pugliese**
In the style of *Puglia*. See *chiocciole, orata, spiedini, timballo, triglie*.

**Pumaruolo/pumaruoro**
(Campania, Sicilia) Tomatoes.

**Punta di vitello**
Breast of veal.

**Puntarelle**
(Lazio) Chicory salad with anchovies, garlic, oil and vinegar.

**(Col) Puntel(l)**
See *risotto*.

**Punt e Mes**
Popular aperitif, a 'point and a half' of bitterness, made by *Carpano*; said to have originated when customers ordered their drinks to their own specification.

**Puorco**
(Sicilia) Pig, pork.

**Pure(a)**
Purée.

**(In) Purgatorio**
See *polpo*.

**Purpetti di milinciani**
(Sicilia) Assorted grilled fish.

**(Alla) Putanesca**
'Strumpet's style'. (Lazio, Campania): With tomatoes, garlic, capers, olives, anchovies, of pasta.

**Putizza**
See *potizza*.

## Quadrello
Rack, of lamb, loin, of pork.

## Quadretti di riso alla piemontese
Rice fritters with meat sauce, cheese, truffle.

## Quadrucci
Tiny pasta cubes, for soup.

## Quagg(h)iaridd (di Andria)
Sheep's offal, sausage and cheese wrapped in caul and baked.

## Quaglie
Quails. *Q. alla borghese*: wrapped in vine leaves and roast, on a bed of puréed peas and lettuce. *Q. rincartate* (Umbria): baked in bread dough.

*Quagliette*: stuffed rolls, parcels, often of cabbage. *Q. di vitello*: veal rolls with ham on skewers.

## Quaietta
(Piemonte) Veal cutlets stuffed with meat, cheese and truffles.

## (Alla) Quaresima/quaresimale
Lenten style, of Lent. Meatless, probably with fish.

## Quartiretto
(Piemonte) Haunch of goat stuffed with spinach and cheese, roast.

## Quartirolo
(Lombardia) Mild smooth square cheese.

## Quarto
Hindquarters, haunch, leg.

## Quatro spezie
Four spices, usually pepper, nutmeg, juniper, cloves.

**Rabarbaro**
Rhubarb.
Dark-coloured aperitif made from rhubarb.

**Raboso**
(Veneto) Red grape variety.

**Radicchio (di Castelfranco/rosso/di Treviso/di Verona)**
Red chicory, with long purple leaves, or fatter and more cabbage-shaped; also known as *rosa, spadone*.

**Rafano**
Horseradish.

**Raffreddato**
Chilled.

**Ragnetto**
(Emilia-Romagna) Small bread roll.

**Ragno di mare**
Spider crab.

**Ragù**
Rich meat sauce to accompany pasta. *R. alla bolognese*: made with veal, ham, vegetables, nutmeg and cream. *R. alla napoletana*: of veal rolls stuffed with cheese, raisins, pine nuts, or of beef, simmered in red wine and tomatoes, the sauce served with pasta and the meat as a separate course; also known as *o'rraù*.

**(Alla) Ragusana**
In the style of Ragusa, *Sicilia*. See *lasagne, trippa*.

**(Al) Ramerino**
See *pannino*.

**Ramitello**
(Molise) Trade name of the Majo Norante winery.

**Ramolaccio**
Horseradish.

**Rane/ranocchi**
Frogs. *R. in guazzetto* (Lombardia, Piemonte): cooked in butter and wine or tomato sauce, with parsley. *R. ripiene* (Piemonte): stuffed with sausage, breadcrumbed and fried. *R. in casseruola alla vercellese*: simmered in white wine with mushrooms and anchovies.
*Rana pescatrice*: monkfish, angler fish.

**Rapata**
(Lombardia) Rice and turnip soup.

**Rape**
Turnips.
*Rape rosse*: beetroot.

**Rascatelli**
See *cavatelli*.

**Rattatuia di frutti di mare alla marchigiana**
Light stew of seafood, tomatoes, wine, served with rice.

**Ravanello**
Radish.

**Ravello**
(Campania) Small town noted for fine non-*DOC* wines, often exported under the Gran Caruso label.

**(Alla) Ravennate**
In the style of Ravenna, *Emilia-Romagna*. See *brodetto*.

**Raviggiolo**
(Umbria, Toscana, Emilia, Marche) Sheep's milk cheese with full flavour.

**Raviotta**
Piquant cold sauce with vinegar and capers.

**Ravioli**
(Liguria) Small pasta cases, square or oval, enclosing a stuffing. See also *calcioni, gravioli*. *R. alla calabrese*: filled with sausage, cheese, egg and served with a sauce and cheese. *R. caprese*: stuffed with cheese, eggs and herbs. *R. genovese*: filled with curd cheese and wild greens, with meat or *pesto* sauce. *R. alla napoletana*: stuffed with ham, *ricotta, mozzarella* and parmesan cheese. *R. trentini*: stuffed with meat and chicken. *R. della Val Pusteria*: made with rye flour, stuffed with spinach, cheese or sauerkraut, sometimes fried.
(Toscana) Small dumplings. *R. alla fiorentina*: of spinach and *ricotta* cheese, boiled and served with parmesan.
(Emilia-Romagna) Sweet pastries filled with marzipan or jam.
*Ravioli dolci* (Liguria): stuffed with beef marrow and candied fruit,

fried and sprinkled with sugar.

*Raviolini*: tiny pasta squares, for soup.

## Razza

Skate, ray.

## Recchiatelle

(Puglia) Small shell-shaped pasta, usually with fish and tomato sauce, the fish itself served as a second course; also known as *ricchielle di magro*.

## Recioto

(Veneto) Wine made from semi-dried grapes collected from the upper parts or 'ears' ('recia' in local dialect) of bunches; sometimes sweet or sparkling, or, when fermented right out, producing strong dry wine, *Amarone*.

## Refosco (del Peduncolo Rosso)

(Friuli-Venezia Giulia) Red grape variety, making heavy strong wines, well-regarded locally.

## Regaleali

(Sicilia) Popular non-*DOC* wines.

## Regina in porchetta

(Umbria) Stuffed carp baked in a wood oven.

## Reginette

(Liguria) Pasta ribbons, for soup.

## Remolazzitt

(Lombardia) Radish.

## Reni

Kidneys.

## Rete/reticella

Pig's caul, often used as a wrapping for other ingredients.

## Rheinriesling

See *Riesling*.

## Ribes

Currants – black, white or red.

## Ribollita

(Toscana) Cabbage and bean soup reheated ('reboiled') or thickened with bread on succeeding days.

## Riccadonna

Major wine and vermouth firm, based on Canelli, *Piemonte*.

## Ricchie 'i prieviti/richielle

See *cavatelli, recchiatelle*.

## Ricci di donna

(Calabria) Spiral pasta shapes, served with a sauce and cheese.

## Ricciarelli

(Toscana) Sweet almond biscuits.

## Ricci di mare

Sea urchins.

## Ricciola

Amberjack, sea fish.
*Ricciolo*: curly endive.
*Ricciolini*: small pasta curls.

**Ricco**
Rich.

**Ricotta**
Soft mild fresh cheese like a white cake, made from reheating ('recooked') the leftover whey of milk; also available salted, smoked and as a hard sharp cheese.

**Ricottone**
(Campania) Confection of cheese, sugar and candied peel.

**Riebl**
(Trentino-Alto Adige) Buckwheat flour fritters.

**Riesling**
*R. italico*: white grape variety grown in the north; also known as *Welschriesling*. *R. renano*: classic white grape inported from the Rhine; also known as *Rheinriesling*.

**Riffato**
Reheated.

**Rigaglie**
Giblets, of fowl.

**Rigato**
Ridged, of pasta shapes. *Grosso rigato/rigat(t)i/rigatoni/rigoletti*: ridged hollow pasta tubes of various sizes.

**Rimestato**
Stirred. Scrambled, of eggs.

**Rincartato**
See *quaglie*.

**Rinforzo**
See *insalata*.

**Riondele**
See *ris*.

**Ripiddu nivicatu**
(Sicilia) 'Black' rice with cuttlefish, topped with *ricotta* cheese and tomato sauce, to resemble Mount Etna.

**Ripieno**
Stuffed. Stuffing. *Ripieni fritti*: triangular fritters with various savoury stuffings.

**(Di) Riposto**
Hidden, secret.

**Riquagghiu**
See *pasta*.

## Ris

Rice. *R. in cagnon(e)* (Piemonte): boiled, finished in butter with cheese and herbs. *R. e fasui/lujanie* (Friuli-Venezia Guilia): thick rice soup with beans or sausage. *R. e riondele* (Piemonte): cooked with mallow leaves and milk.

## Risada

(Piemonte) Rice and beans in red wine.

## Riserva

Reserve, applied to *DOC* and *DOCG* wines after a specified period of ageing.

## Risetto

(Marche) Croquettes of tiny anchovies and sardines.

## Risi/riso

Rice. *Risi e bisi* (Veneto): thick rice soup with peas. *R. in cavroman* (Veneto): cooked with lamb and spices. *R. con la ua alla veneziana*: with grapes, garlic, cheese. *Riso alla canavesana*: boiled in meat broth, finished with *fontina, grana* and Emmenthal cheese. *R. arrosto alla genovese*: baked with veal or sausage, artichokes or peas and parmesan. *R. alla lamonese*: with butter, cheese, beans. *R. ricco*: boiled, with creamy cheese sauce. *R. alla ristori*: with cabbage, bacon, sausage. *R. al forno in pevareda alla rovigina*: baked with chicken livers, mushrooms, anchovies. *R. e tardura* (Emilia-Romagna): finished with beaten egg and cheese.

## Risot cui croz

(Friuli-Venezia Giulia) Rice with frogs.

## Risotto

Creamy mass of rice cooked slowly to absorb the broth, with various ingredients added; a dish in its own right, served alone (with one exception). *R. al Barolo* (Piemonte): cooked in *Barolo* and broth, served with butter and cheese. *R. cacuòcciuoli* (Sicilia): with beans, peas, artichokes and cheese. *R. alla campagnola* (Lombardia): with beans, tomatoes, sausage. *R. alla certosina*: with prawns, mushrooms, peas, perhaps perch, frogs. *R. alla fiorentina*; with meat sauce and chicken giblets. *R. alla chioggiotta*: with gobies, white wine and parmesan. *R. mantovano*: with chicken livers and sage. *R. alla milanese*: with chicken broth and saffron, sometimes white wine or *marsala* plus ham and beef marrow, with cheese and butter added; served with *ossobuco*, the only time *risotto* accompanies another dish. *R. alla monzese*: with sausage and tomato sauce. *R. alla napoletana*: with ham, tomatoes, butter and parmesan. *R. nero* (Toscana, Veneto): 'black' with cuttlefish and the ink. *R. alla novarese*: finished in a frying pan with onion and wine, butter and cheese. *R. padovano*: with veal, chicken livers, peas. *R. alla parmigiana*: in broth, with butter and parmesan added. *R. alla piemontese*: with giblets and sausage, or meat sauce and truffles. *R. alla pilota* (Lombardia): with fried sausage and cheese at the end. *R. polesano*: with eel, mullet and bass. *R. col puntel* (Lombardia): 'with a support' of pork chops; also known as *puntell*. *R. al/in salto* (Lombardia): cooked, formed into a thick round and fried. *R. alla sbirraglia* (Veneto): with chicken broth and bits. *R. alla siciliana*: with beans, peas, artichokes. *R. al tajo* (Veneto): with prawns and eel. R. *alla toscana*: with beef, calf's kidney and liver, tomatoes. R. *alla trevigiana*: with sausage, onions, celery. R. *alla valtellinese*: with beans, cabbage and sage. R. *verde*: with spinach. R. *alla veronese*: with ham and mushrooms, or fried fish.

### Ristorante

Restaurant. Restorative, refreshing. See also *riso*.

### Ristretto

Strong, concentrated, especially of soup.

### Riviera del Garda Bresciano

(Lombardia) *DOC* zone on Lake Garda, known for dry red wine and *Chiaretto*.

### (Alla) Rivierasca

'Coastal style'. See *branzino*.

### Robiola

(Lombardia, Piemonte) Soft rich white cheese pressed into square or circular form, with a delicate fragrance and taste when young; often mashed and steeped in oil.

*Robiolina*: spicier version, sometimes with goat or sheep's milk added.

### Rocciata di Assisi

Pastry layered with nuts, raisins, dried figs, prune.

### Rognon(cin)i

Kidneys. R. *di vitello alla fiorentina*: calf's, baked in butter with herbs and lemon. R. *alla veneziana*: with Marsala.

### Rognoso

See *frittata*.

## Role

Roll, of veal, beef, usually braised, served hot or cold.
*Rollatini*: Little rolls, e.g. of veal.

## Romagna

*DOC* region for 3 wines named according to grape variety.

## (Alla) Romagnola

In the style of *Romagna*. See *agnello, anitra, castagne, lenticchie, piadina, polenta, salsiccia, spezzatino, tagliatelle, tortelloni.*

## (Alla) Romana

In the style of Rome, *Lazio*. See *agnello, animelle, broccoli, brodetto, carciofi, crostata, fagioli, fave, gnocchi, lattuga, lumache, menta, minestra, pecorino, peperoni, pizza, pollo, saltimbocca, sarde, seppie, spezzatino, spiedini, spinaci, stracciatella, trippa, zucchine.*

## Rombo

Turbot. Brill.

## Rondinella

Flying fish.

## Rondino

Pomfret, sea fish.

## Rosa

See *radicchio.*

## Rosada

(Trentino-Alto Adige) Sweet almond custard.

**Rosato**
Rosé, of wine.

**Roscioli**
(Abruzzo) Red mullet. *R. sul focone alla pescatora*: cooked in a special brick box over an open fire with hot pepper.

**Rosetta**
See *michetta*.

**Rosmarino**
Rosemary, the herb.

**Rosolio**
Red rose-flavoured liqueur.

**Rospa/rospo**
Monkfish.

**(Alla) Rossanese**
In the style of Rossano, *Calabria*. See *melanzane*.

**Rossese**
(Liguria) Red grape variety.

**Rossetti**
Goby, tiny fish.

**Rosso**
Red. See also *radicchio*.
*Rosso antico*: wine-based aperitif with herbs.

**Rosso Cònero**
(Marche) Robust red *DOC* wine based on *Montepulciano* grapes grown around Monte Conero.

**Rosso Piceno**
(Marche) Dry red *DOC* wine grown in considerable quantity, mainly from *Sangiovese* and *Montepulciano* grapes.

**Rosticceria**
Delicatessen, often with snack bar.

**Rosticini**
(Abruzzo) Grilled skewered lamb or pork.

**Rostida**
(Piemonte) Pork offal stewed with tomato and *polenta*.

**Rostin negaa**
(Lombardia) Veal chops finished in white wine.

**Rostisciada**
(Lombardia) Pork and sausage stew with tomatoes and wine.

**Rostissana**
(Emilia-Romagna) Courgettes simmered with onions and peppers.

**Rotelle/rotelloni**
Spiral pasta shapes.

**Rotolo**
Roll.

**Rotto**
Broken.

**Rovello**
Blue-spotted sea bream.

**Roventini alla toscana**
Fried pig's blood with parmesan.

**Rovi**
Blackberries.

**(Alla) Rovigana**
In the style of Rovigo, *Veneto*. See *riso*.

**Rovinassi/rovinazzi**
(Veneto) Chicken bits and giblets, often with rice or pasta.

**Rubino di Cantavenna**
(Piemonte) Dry red *DOC* wine based on *Barbera* grapes.

**Ruccul**
(Basilicata) Pizza with garlic, herbs and hot pepper.

**Ruffino**
Prominent shippers of *Chianti* wine.

**Ruländer**
See *Pinot*.

**Ruote di carro**
Pasta in the shape of 'cartwheels'.

**Russo**
Russian. See *insalata*.

**Russole**
Type of fungus.

**Rustico**
'Rustic'. *Rustici con tartufi* (Piemonte): small light pastries stuffed with truffles. See also *pizza*.

**Rustida**
See *polenta*.

## Sabbioso
See *patate.*

## Sacchetto
Sea perch.

## Sa corda
See *cordula.*

## (Alla) Saffi
See *maccheroni.*

## Sagne chine
(Calabria) Pasta sheets layered with meat balls, eggs, cheese, vegetables and finished in the oven.

## Sagnette
(Abruzzo) Square-section pasta noodles. *S. all'aquilina*: with ham and tomatoes.

## Sagrantino
(Umbria) Red grape variety.

## Salama (da sugo)
(Emilia-Romagna) Sausage of pork, spices and wine, eaten hot with purée potato; also known as *salame de succo.*

## Salame
Salami, raw salt-cured sausage with numerous regional varieties, mild or strong, fresh or matured. *S.d'la duja* (Piemonte): soft and mild, preserved in fat in a special pot ('duja'); also known as *salamin d'la duja. S. fabriano*: of pork and beef. *S. di Felino*: pure pork in an uneven shape. *S.fiorentina*: pure pork, large and coarse cut. *S. alla friulana*: sautéed slices with vinegar, eaten hot with *polenta. S. genovese*: made of beef, pork and pork fat, quite strong. *S. gentile* (Emilia-Romagna): lean pork with black peppercorns. *S. milano*: made of pork lean and fat and beef, pepper, garlic and white wine, mass produced and widely exported; also known as *crespone. S. napoletano*: similar to the Milan version but more peppery. *S. sardo*: flavoured with red pepper. *S. ungherese*: Hungarian recipe, of finely chopped pork, beef and pork fat.

Sausage-type roll, loaf, e.g. of tuna.

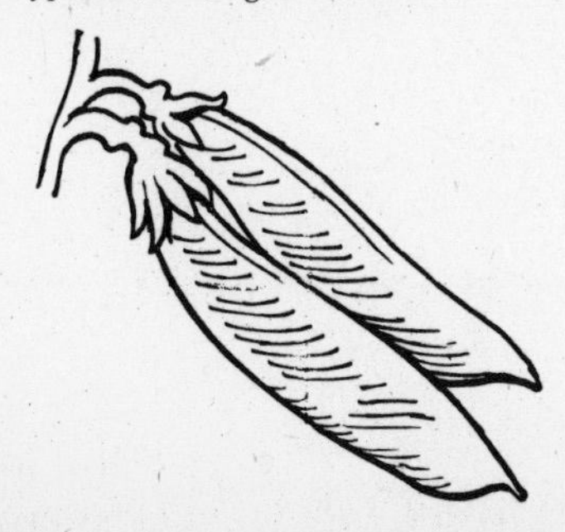

**Salamin**
See *salame*.

**Salamoia**
Brine, pickle.

**Salatina**
Fresh salad greens.

**Salato**
Salted meats, salami. Salted, savoury.

**Salcrauto**
(Trentino-Alto Adige) Sauerkraut.

**Sale**
Salt. *S. grosso*: coarse salt.

**Salice Salentino**
(Puglia) Town making red and rosé wines based on *Negroamaro* grapes; the rosé sometimes labelled 'Prodotto Invecchiato' after 1 year ageing.

**Salini**
(Trentino-Alto Adige) Stick-shaped roll with coarse salt and cummin seeds.

**(In) Salmì**
In a rich wine sauce, usually of game. See also *sardine*.

**Salmistrato**
Pickled, cured in brine.

**Salmone**
Salmon.

**(Al) Salmoriglio**

(Calabria, Sicilia) Dressed with oil, lemon juice, parsley and oregano, especially of grilled swordfish.

**Salpa**

Sea bream.

**Salsa**

Sauce. *S. inglese*: Worcestershire sauce. *S. de noxe* (Liguria): walnut and pine nut sauce, for pasta. *S. verde*: cold green sauce, with herbs, perhaps garlic, anchovies, pine nuts.

*Salsetta*: light sauce, salad dressing.

**Salsiccia**

Sausage. *S. di filottrano* (Marche): cooked in white wine and meat sauce, served with potato. *S. leccese*: of veal and pork with lemon peel and spices. *S. di Nicosia*: strong pork and rabbit mixture. *Salsicce alla romagnola*: fried, with sage and tomato sauce.

**Saltato**

Sautéed. See also *maccheroni*.

**Saltimbocca (alla romana)**

Thin veal slices rolled with ham and sage, sautéed in butter and finished in white wine. *S. alla marchigiana*: of beef, bacon and ham. *S. alla partenopea*: of veal, ham, cheese, with tomato sauce.

**(In) Salto**

Flipped over, fried.

**Salume**

Salt pork.

*Salumeria*: delicatessen.

*Salumi*: salted meats.

**Salvia**

Sage, the herb.

**Sambuca**

Clear liqueur from witch elder, tasting of aniseed.

**(Alla) Sammartinese**

St Martin's style. See *vermicelli*.

**Sancele**

(Sicilia) Black pudding of pig's blood, raisins, sugar and spices, sliced and fried with onions.

**(Di) San Daniele**

Of San Daniele, *Friuli*. See *prosciutto*.

**San Gimignano**

(Toscano) Town celebrated for dry white *DOC* wine made from local *Vernaccia* grapes.

**San Giovanniello**
See *maccheroni.*

**Sangiovese**
Red grape variety grown throughout the country, particularly important in *Chianti, Montalcino* and *Montepulciano.*

**Sangue**
Blood.

**Sangue di Giuda**
(Lombardia) 'Blood of Judas'. Red *DOC* wine, usually quite fizzy.

**Sanguinaccio**
Blood sausage, black pudding. See also *migliaccio.*

**San Giuseppe**
St Joseph See *bignè, fritelle.*

**San Martino della Battaglia**
(Lombardia) Village producing high-quality dry white *DOC* wine from *Tocai* grapes, most of it consumed locally.

**San Pietro**
St Peter. See *pesce.*

**(Di) San Secondo**
Of San Secondo, *Emilia Romagna.* See *spalla.*

**San Severo**
(Puglia) Red, white and rosé wines *(DOC).*

**San Siro**
See *pane.*

**Santa Chiara**
See *facciuni, pagnotta.*

**Santa Maddalena**
(Trentino-Alto Adige) Famous red *DOC* wine.

**Sant'Anna di Isola Capo Rizzuto**
(Calabria) Dry red *DOC* wine based on *Gaglioppo* grapes.

**(In) Saor**
(Veneto) Soused, of fish, i.e. fried then marinated in oil etc., with pine nuts, sultanas and lemon peel added.

**Sapore**
Taste, flavour. *Ai sapori*: with herbs. *Saporito*: tasty.

**Saraceno**
Buckwheat.

**Saraghine**
(Romagna) Fish similar to sardine or anchovies.

## Sarago

Sea bream.

## (Alla) Sarda

In the style of *Sardegna*. See *agnello, anitra, coratella, filetto, manzo, minestrone, pecorino, pernice, polenta, pomodori, salame, vitello, zuppa*.

## Sardegna

Island and wine region, with 16 *DOC*'s mostly named according to grape variety, only 3 having the general designation *Sardegna*.

## Sard(ell)e

Sardines. *S. a beccaficcu* (Sicilia): fried with anchovies, pine nuts, raisins and finished in the oven. *S. alla catanese*: deep fried with cheese and herbs. *S. alla cetrarese*: baked with oil and herbs. *S. alla contadina*: fried, with tomatoes and herbs. *S. fritte alla genovese/alla ligure*: stuffed with mushrooms, herbs, cheese and fried. *S. alla marchigiana*: marinated with herbs and baked. *S. alla messinese*: finished in tomato sauce with capers and olives. *S. alla napoletana*: baked with oil, herbs and tomatoes. *S. ripiene alla palermitana*: stuffed with raisins, nuts, anchovies and spices, baked. *S. ripiene alla romana*: stuffed with spinach and cream, deep fried. *S. in tortiera*: baked with parsely, garlic oil and vinegar.

## Sardena(i)ra

(Liguria) Flat bread with onions, black olives, tomatoes, cheese and anchovies; also known as *pissaladeira, pizza all'Aandrea/alla genovese*.

## Sardine/sardoni

Sardines. *S. in salmi* (Sardegna): baked with tomatoes, herbs, oil and vinegar. *S. a scotadeo* (Veneto): charcoal-grilled, with lemon.

## Sargo/sarpa

Sea bream.

**Sartu (di riso)**
(Campania) Baked rice mould filled with meat balls, sausage, giblets, mushrooms, cheese, peas and tomato sauce.

**Sasizzeddi**
(Sicilia) Veal rolls stuffed with cheese and sausage.

**Sas melicheddas**
(Sardegna) Almond biscuits.

**(Alla) Sassarese**
In the style of Sassari, *Sardegna*. See *ciciones, monzittas*.

**Sassella**
See *Valtellina*.

**Sassicaia**
(Toscana) Non-*DOC* red wine made from *Cabernet* grapes by Marchese Mario Incisa della Rochetta, marketed by *Antinori*; one of Italy's finest reds.

**Sassolino**
(Emilia-Romagna) Pork sausage, served hot with potatoes or lentils.
Liqueur.

**Saticulano**
See *caso forte*.

**Sauerbraten**
(Trentino-Alto Adige) Meat stew with vinegar.

**Sauerkraut**
(Trentino-Alto Adige) Cabbage fermented with spices.

**Saursuppe**
(Trentino-Alto Adige) Tripe soup.

**Saussa d'avì**
(Piemonte) Honey, nut and mustard sauce, for boiled meats.

**Sauvignon**
White grape variety, native of Bordeaux, increasingly important in the north.

**Savarino**
Ring-shaped yeast cake.

**(Alla) Savoi(ard)a**
In the style of Savoia, *Piemonte*. See *frittata, trippa, trota*.
*Savoiardi*: sponge fingers.

**Savuto**
(Calabria) *DOC* area for dry red and rosé wines.

**Sbira**
(Liguria) Stewed tripe with cheese and meat sauce.

**(Alla) Sbirraglia**
'Police-style'. See *risotto*.

**Sbricciolono/sbrisolano**
See *torta*.

**Sburrità**
(Elba) Fish stew.

**Scacciata**
(Sicilia) Light pastry, filled with cheese, tomatoes and anchovy or pork, or with sweetened *ricotta* cheese.

**Scalcione**
See *focaccia*.

**Scaligero**
See *zuppa*.

**Scalmarita/scammarita**
(Umbria, Lazio) Smoked pork sausage with fennel seeds.

**Scalogni**
Shallots.

**Scalopp(in)e**
Escalopes, thin slices especially of veal, cut across the grain and flattened, usually fried and served with a sauce. *S. alla livornese*: with Marsala sauce and parsley. *S. alla perugina*: fried, with chicken liver croutons. *S. alla triestina*: breadcrumbed and fried, garnished with lemon, anchovy, olives.

## Scamorza
(Campania) Firm fresh pear-shaped cheese with delicate flavour, usually of cow's but also of buffalo's or goat's milk, similar to *mozzarella*.

## Scampi
Scampi, Dublin Bay prawns, particularly from the Adriatic; misleadingly used for any kind of prawn. *S. alla veneziana*: cold, dressed with oil and lemon.

## Scandiano
(Emilia-Romagna) Small town known for white *DOC* wine based on *Sauvignon* grapes; may be dry or semi-sweet and sparkling.

## Scanno
(Abruzzo) Variety of *pecorino* cheese.

## (A) Scapece
(Sicilia, Calabria, Campania, Abruzzo, Puglia) Soused, of fish, fried, then marinated in oil vinegar, garlic and herbs. *S. alla vastese/di Vasto*: applied to skate or dogfish, plus saffron.
Pickled, of vegetables.

## Scarcedda
(Puglia) Nut bread.

## Scarol(ell)a
Escarole, salad green.

## Scarpazzone
See *erbazzone*.

## Scarpena
(Veneto) Rascasse, scorpion fish.

## Scaveccio alla grossetana
Eel marinated in oil, vinegar and hot pepper.

## Scelto
Choice, select, exquisite. *A scelta*: of your choice.

## Scherpelle
See *pèttole*.

## Schiabacheddu
(Sicilia) Tiny fish.

## Schiacciata/schiacciato
(Emilia-Romagna, Puglia) Flat bread or bread rolls; also known as *stria*.

## Schiaff(ett)oni
(Calabria, Campania) Ravioli- or macaroni-type pasta.

## Schiava
(Trentino-Alto Adige) Red grape variety; also known as *Vernatsch*.

## Schidionato/(allo) schidione
Spit-roasted.

## Schila
(Veneto) Shrimp.

## Schinco
(Friuli) Braised whole shin of veal with anchovies.

## Schiodionata
Spit-roasted dish.

## Schissoeula
(Lombardia) Rustic flat bread with raisins and pork bits; also known as *chisöl*.

## Schmorbraten
(Trentino-Alto Adige) Beef marinated then braised in wine, herbs and tomatoes.

## Schneckensuppe
(Trentino-Alto Adige) Snail soup.

## Sciabola
See *pesce*.

## Scialcione
See *focaccia*.

## Sciantigliè
(Lazio) Sweetened whipped cream, served with biscuits.

**Sciarrano**
Sea perch.

**Sciatt**
(Lombardia) Buckwheat pancakes with *grappa* and cheese.

**Scilatielli**
See *filatelli*.

**Sciroppo**
Syrup. *Sciroppato*: sweetened, in syrup.

**Sciutte**
(Liguria) Almond sweets.

**Sciule piene**
(Piemonte) Baked onion rings stuffed with macaroons, sultanas and spices.

**Sciumette**
(Liguria) Sweet mousse served with custard.

**(A) Sciusciareddu**
See *capretto*.

**Sciuscieddu**
(Sicilia) Soup thickened with egg, cheese, herbs and breadcrumbs, sometimes finished in the oven like a soufflé.

**Scivateddi**
(Calabria) Thin spaghetti with pork sauce and smoked *ricotta* cheese.

**(Di) Scoglio**
Of the rocks.

**Sconciglio**
(Calabria) Murex, small shellfish.

**Scorfan(ott)o**
Scorpion fish, rascasse.

**Scorz(ett)a**
Peel, of lemon, orange.

**Scorzonera**
Scorzonera, oyster plant.

**(A) Scotadeo**
See *sardoni*.

**(A) Scottadito**
See *costolette*.

**Scottiglia**
(Toscana) Rich stew of veal, poultry, pork and game.

**Scrigno di Venere**
Large shells of pasta with a stuffing.

**Scripelle 'mbusse/'nfuss**
(Abruzzo) Pancakes layered with cheese, served with chicken broth and cheese.

**Scroccafusi**
(Marche) Small sweet cakes.

**Scumuni**
(Sicilia) Chocolate or pistachio ice cream with a centre of beaten egg.

**Sebadas**
(Sardegna) Cheese and honey fritters.

**Secco**
Dry, dried.

**Secole**
(Veneto) Scraps of raw beef or veal, often added to rice.

**Secondo**
According to. *S. grandezza/SG*: priced according to size, e.g. of steak. *S. stagione*: available in season.

*Secondi*: Second, main, course of a meal, i.e. meat, poultry, game or fish.

**Sedano**
Celery. *Sedani alla pratese*: stuffed with veal and chicken livers, deep fried and finished in the oven with meat sauce.

*Sedano-rapa/di Verona*: celeriac, celery root.

*Sedani*: ridged pasta tubes.

**Segale**
Rye. Rye loaf.

**Segreto**
Secret.

**Segrigeula**
(Lombardia) Wild thyme.

**Seirass del Lausùn**
(Piemonte) Curd cheese in linen bags.

**Sella**
Saddle, of lamb, veal.

**Sella & Mosca**
(Sardegna) Important company of wine-makers based in Alghero.

**Sèller**
(Lombardia) Celery.

**Selvaggina**
Game.

**Selvatico**
Wild, uncultivated.

**Sementare**
Tiny eels.

**Semi**
Seeds. *S. di papavero*: poppy seeds.
*Semi d'orzo/semini*: tiny pasta grains, for soup.
Semi, half. *Semi-secco*: medium sweet, usually of sparkling wine. *Semidure*: soft-boiled, of eggs. *Semifreddo*: mousse, chilled pudding.

**Semolino**
Semolina, durum wheat.

**(Alla) Semplice**
Simply.

**Semuda/semuta**
(Lombardia) Piquant cheese.

**Senape**
Mustard. *S. di Digione*: Dijon mustard.

**(Alla) Senese**
In the style of Siena, *Toscana*. See *petto*.

**Seppie**
Cuttlefish. *S. alla gradese*: fried with herbs and finished in white wine. *S. ripiene alla pesarese*: stuffed with garlic, capers and anchovies, stewed. *S. alla romana*: simmered with white wine, anchovies, garlic. *S. alla veneziana*: stewed in their own ink and white wine, served with *polenta*.
*Seppiol(in)e*: small cuttlefish.

**Serpe**
(Marche) Almond cake in a roll.

**Serpentaria**
Tarragon.

**Serra**
Greenhouse.

**Serrapetrona**
(Marche) Village known for *Vernaccia di S.*: rare red sparkling *DOC* wine, dry or sweet.

**Servizio**
Service, service charge.

**Sesamo**
Sesame seed.

**Settesoli**
(Sicilia) Major wine cooperative at Menfi.

**Sfilato**
Boned and jointed, in small pieces, of rabbit, hare.

**Sfilatino**
(Toscana) Bread loaf.

**Sfincione/sfinciuni**
(Sicilia) Thick soft pizza topped with tomatoes, anchovies, cheese, olives.

**Sfogie**
(Veneto) Sole, the fish.

## Sfogliata

Flaky pastry.

(Puglia) Baked roll of yeast dough stuffed with anchovies, olives, cheese.

*Sfogliatelle* (Campania): flaky pastry layered with *ricotta* cheese, spices and candied fruit.

*Sfogliatine ripiene* (Liguria): pastry fritters filled with chard, eggs and cheese.

## Sformat(in)o

Mould, of vegetables, rice. Dessert brick.

## Sforzato/Sfursat

(Lombardia) Strong dark red wine made from semi-dried grapes.

## SG

See *secondo*.

## Sgombro

Mackerel. *S. alla calabrese*: grilled over coals, with anchovy paste.

## Sguazeto a la bechèra

(Veneto) Stew of ox tripe, tail and other offal, with Parmesan.

## Sguazzarotti

See *tortelli*.

## (Alla) Siciliana

In the style of *Sicilia*. With anchovies, sultanas, pine nuts and vinegar, of fish, vegetables. See also *aragosta, broccoli, cassata, cassettine, costolette, frittata, insalata, melanzane, olive, pecorino, pernice, risotto, stoccafisso, tonno, triglia*.

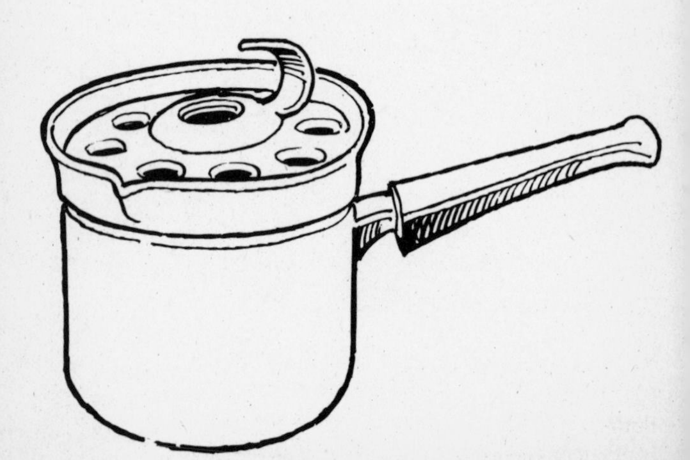

**Signore**
See *filetto*.
*Signorini*: tiny pink fish, usually fried.

**Silvestro**
See *Centerbe*.

**Simbula**
See *pane*.

**Simmuledda alla foggiana**
Potato and fennel soup thickened with buckwheat flour.

**Sinisc(hiell)o**
(Calabria) Curled octopus.

**(De) Siouri**
(Piemonte) See *polenta*.

**Siracusa**
(Sicilia) City with *DOC* for rare dessert wine made from *Moscato* grapes.

**(Alla) Siracusana**
In the style of Siracuse, *Sicilia*. See *spaghetti*.

**(Al) Sivè**
See *lepre*.

**Sizzano**
(Piemonte) Red *DOC* wine, based on *Nebbiolo* grapes.

**Smacafam**
(Trentino-Alto Adige) *Polenta* with bacon and sausage, or with sultanas, nuts and aniseed.

**Smann**
(Friuli-Venezia Giulia) Sweet omelette.

**Smegiazza**
(Veneto) *Polenta* cake with pine nuts, raisins, treacle, etc.

**Smeriglio**
Shark.

**(Alla) Smolz**
See *fagioli*.

**Soare**
(Veneto) Grape, pear and apple jam.

**Soave**
(Veneto) Small town renowned for dry white *DOC* wine from *Garganega* grapes.

**Sode**
Hard-boiled, of eggs.

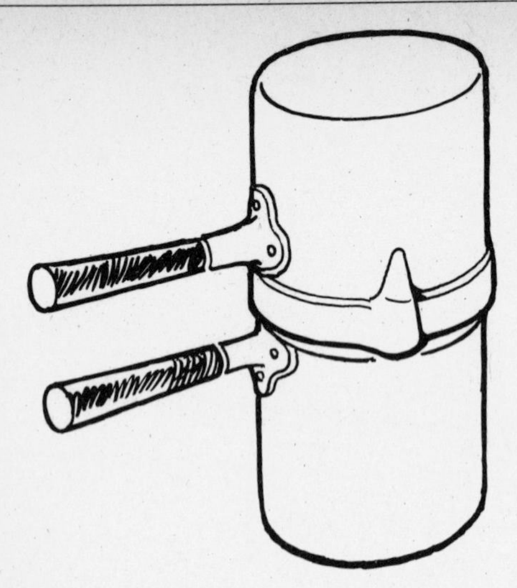

**Sofegao**
(Veneto) Cooked slowly in a closed pot with little liquid.

**Soffiato**
Soufflé.

**Soffritto**
Basis of a soup or stew. Sauce, for pasta. *S. calabrese*: lamb's offal with herbs, tomatoes, hot pepper, spread on flat bread; also known as *suffritu*. See also *zuppa*.

**Sogliola**
Sole, flat sea fish. *S. alla veneziana*: stuffed with herbs and grilled, with wine sauce.

**Solopaca**
(Campania) Town with *DOC* for red and white wines.

**(In) Solsa**
See *tordi*.

**Soma d'aii**
(Piemonte) Garlic toast.

**Sopa**
(Veneto) Soup. *S. coada*: of pigeon, bread, wine. *S. de fasoi*: of salt pork and beans.

**Soppressa**
Sausage. *S. del Pasubio*: firm textured pork with potatoes and chestnuts.
*Soppressata* (Molise, Puglia, Calabria): roughly cut, of pork and bacon plus herbs. *S. di Fabriano*: smooth, smoked, of pork and spices.

## Sorni
(Trentino-Alto Adige) Light red *DOC* wine.

## Sorpresine
Tiny pasta shapes, for soup.

## (Alla) Sorrentina
In the style of Sorrento, *Campania*. With tomatoes and olives. Mixed with tomato and cheese sauce, plus grated cheese, of pasta.

## Sorsi-Sennori
(Sardegna) *DOC* for sweet dessert wine made from *Moscato* grapes.

## Sos coricheddos
(Sardegna) Heart-shaped almond biscuits.

## Sospiri
Small cheese custards.

## Sotto/sott'
Under, in. *Sottaceti*: pickles.

## Sottile
Thin, fine, delicate.

## Soupe
(Valle d'Aosta) Soup. *S. cogneintze*: of rye bread, cheese and meat broth. *S.valpellinentze*: of bread, cabbage and cheese in a meat broth.

## Spaccadenti
(Toscana) Almond biscuits.

## Spaccatina
(Abruzzo) Bread loaf. See also *ciope*.

## Spada
See *pesce*.

## Spadone
See *radicchio*.

## Spaghetti
Spaghetti, long thin pasta strands. *S. alla Bellini* (Sicilia): with tomatoes, aubergines, and *ricotta* cheese; after the composer, a native of Sicily, and also known as *S. con la Norma* from his famous opera. *S. alla carlofortina*: with tuna, anchovies, olives. *S. alla catanese*: with aubergines, cheese, hot pepper. *S. alla napoletana*: with mushrooms, tongue and tomatoes. *S. alla palermitana*: with anchovies, tomatoes, olives, capers. *S. alla siracusana*: with anchovies and olives.

*Spaghettini*: thin spaghetti. *S. alla carrettiera*: with basil, tomato and garlic sauce.

## Spalla
Shoulder, of veal, lamb, etc.

*Spalla di San Secondo*: cured shoulder of pork.

**Spanna**
(Piemonte) Name for *Nebbiolo* grape; used for many fine non-*DOC* red wines.

**Spanocchi**
Large prawns.

**Sparaglione**
Small sea bream.

**Sparasi**
(Veneto) Asparagus.

**Sparnocchi**
(Toscana) Scampi.

**Specchie**
See *pesce*.

**Speck**
(Alto Adige) Smoke-cured ham, with herbs and spices, usually served in slices with black bread.

**Spezie**
Spices.

**Spezzat(in)o**
Light stew, sauté finished with a sauce, of 'cut up' meat, often chicken. *S. di coniglio alla ciociara*: of rabbit, with ham, white wine, tomatoes. *S. di c. alla romana*: similar, with Marsala. *S. di pollo alla piemontese*: of chicken, with wine, tomato and truffle sauce, served with rice. *S. di p. alla romagnola*: sautéed, with the wine and herb marinade as sauce. *S. di p. alla trasteverina*: with bacon, wine, tomatoes, mushrooms, peppers, courgettes. *S. di vitello alla bolzanese*: of veal, with tomatoes, paprika and sage.

**(In) Spicchi**
In segments, divided.

**(Allo) Spied(in)o**
On a skewer, spit. Spit-roasted.
*Spiedini*: brochettes, skewers of meat, chicken, sea food etc. *S. alla romana/all' uccelletto*: veal, with bacon, sage and white wine. *S. di allodole alla pugliese*: larks, with mushrooms and sage.
Twisted grooved pasta tubes.

**Spigola**
Sea bass.

**Spinaci**
Spinach. *S. alla milanese*: finished with butter and pine nuts, or served with scrambled eggs. *S. alla piemontese*: with garlic and anchovies. *S. alla romana*: with garlic, ham, pine nuts and raisins. *S. in padella alla trasteverina*; cooked in fat with raisins and pine nuts.

## Spinarolo
Shark.

## Spinola
Sea bass.

## (Alla) Spoletina
In the style of Spoleto, *Umbria. See piccione.*

## Sponga(r)da
(Lombardia) Flat bread served with sausage; or rich honey cake with nuts, raisins, candied fruit and spices.

## Spongata
(Emilia-Romagna, Liguria) Sweet pastry filled with honey, nuts, raisins, candied fruit.

(Sicilia) Rich mixed ice cream with liqueur.

## Spremuto
Squeezed, of oranges, etc. *Spremuta*: (lemon) squash.

## Sproccolati
(Campania) Dried figs stuffed with fennel seeds.

## Spuma
Mousse.

*Spumante*: foaming, frothy. Sparkling, of wine. *(Allo) spumante*: with sparkling wine.

## Spumone
(Campania) Light frothy brick-shaped ice cream with fruit and nuts.

**Spuntature**
(Marche) Lamb's intestine cured in the sun with hot pepper.

**Squadro**
Angel shark, angel fish.

**Squaquaron**
(Emilia-Romagna) Soft delicate version of *stracchino* cheese.

**Squinzano**
(Puglia) Town producing red and rosé *DOC* wines based on *Negroamaro* grapes.

**Stagione**
Season. *Stagionato*: ripe, mature, of cheese.

**(Alla) Stallina**
'Stable-style'. (Lazio) With bacon and garlic, of pasta.

**Stambecco**
Wild goat.

**Starna**
Partridge.

**(Alle) Stecche**
On skewers. *Stecchi*: skewers, usually of savoury ingredients egg-and-breadcrumbed and fried. *S. alla bolognese*: of veal, sausage, cheese and bread. *S. alla genovese*: a selection from chicken livers, sweetbreads, brains, cockscombs, tongue, cheese, artichokes, mushrooms. *S. alla ligure*: pastries stuffed with veal, herbs, cheese. *S. alla mosiana*: sausage, ham, cheese, olives, gherkins, cold as a first course. *S. alla napoletana*: aubergines, tomatoes, cheese and bread.

**Stellette/stelline**
Tiny 'stars' of pasta, for soup.

**Stiacciata**
(Umbria) Baked round of yeast dough topped with cheese, eggs, truffles.

**Stigghioli**
(Calabria, Sicilia) Goat's or lamb's intestines stuffed with the offal, grilled.

**(Alla) Stimpirata**
(Sicilia) With onions, celery, capers and vinegar, of fried fish, especially swordfish.

**Stinchetti**
(Umbria) Small almond meringues.

**Stinco**
Shank, of veal. *S. di vitello alla vicentina*: roasted whole.

**Stivaletti**
Small pasta shapes.

**Stoccafisso**
Dried cod. *S. accomodato* (Liguria): stewed with anchovies, pine nuts, olives and potatoes; also known as *stocche accumudou. S. all' anconetana*: with tomatoes, herbs, perhaps anchovies and potatoes. *S. brand de cujun* (Liguria): boiled and creamed with potatoes, oil and garlic. *S. alla siciliana*: stewed with wine, tomatoes, potatoes, capers, olives, pine nuts, raisins. *S. alla vicentina*: stewed with milk, wine, anchovies, served with *polenta*. See also *burrida*.

**Stock**
Large company of distillers in Trieste, *Friuli-Venezia Giulia*, most famous for its brandy *Stock 84*.

**Storione**
Sturgeon.

**Stortini**
Small pasta crescents, for soup.

**Straca dent**
(Emilia-Romagna) Sweet almond biscuits.

**Stracchino**
(Lombardia) Smooth even yellow cheese with a full smell and flavour.

**Stracci di Antrodoco**
Pancakes layered with meat, vegetables and cheese.

**Stracciatella (alla romana)**
Consommé with 'rags' of beaten egg, semolina and parmesan.

**Stracciato**
Scrambled, of eggs. *Stracciata*: finely shredded lettuce leaves, as a garnish for soup.

**Stracotto**
Braised, stewed. (Toscana, Emilia-Romagna) Braised beef, stew, pot roast. *S. alla fiorentina*: braised beef with herbs, red wine, tomatoes.

**Strangolapreti/strangulapreuti/stran(o)golaprièveti/strangugli/strangugliaprièviti**
'Priest stranglers'. (Basilicata, Campania, Calabria) Small dumplings of potato or flour, sometimes with spinach, served simply or with meat or tomato sauce.

**Strapazzato**
Scrambled, of eggs.

**Strascinati**
(Umbria) Macaroni. *S. alla maniera di Cascia*: with sausage, pork and white wine sauce. *S. alla maniera di Foggia*: with cauliflower, meat sauce and cheese.
(Calabria) Mixed fried peppers, onions, aubergines, courgettes and potatoes.

**Stravecchio(ne)**
Very old, of wine, cheese.

**Strega**
Bright yellow herby liqueur.

**Stria**
See *schiacciata*.

**Stricchetti**
(Emilia-Romagna) Small bow-shaped pasta often served with ham and peas.

**Stringozzi**
(Umbria) Short noodles served with oil and garlic.

**Strinù**
(Lombardia) Beef and pork sausage, usually grilled.

**Strozzapreti all fiorentina**
Spinach and cheese dumplings with meat sauce.

**Strudel**
(Friuli-Venezia Giulia) Flaky pastry layered with fruit, cheese, custard or other ingredients; also known as *stuc(c)olo*.

**Struffoli**
(Campania) Sweet ring-shaped fritters soaked in honey.

**Strutto**
Lard, pork fat.

**Stuc(c)olo**
See *strudel*.

**Stufat(in)o**
Braised, stewed. Stew, usually of beef with red wine, ham, tomatoes etc.
*S. di fave alla bolognese*: broad beans cooked with meat sauce and sausage, served on fried bread.

**Stuffau**
See *ghisau*.

**Suacia**
Scaldfish, flat sea fish.

**Succhittu de conillu**
(Sardegna) Rabbit stew with herbs, olives, capers.

**Succu tundu**
See *fregula*.

**Su farri/farru**
(Sardegna) Mint, cheese and barley soup; also known as *farro*.

**Suffritu**
See *soffritto*.

**Sugarello/sugherello**
Horse mackerel.

**Sughitti**
(Marche) Grape must sweets.

**Sugna**
(Campania) Rendered pork fat.

## Sugo

Sauce, usually of meat and for pasta. *S. finto*: 'pretend' – of vegetables, herbs, mushrooms, tomatoes.

(Emilia-Romagna) Beef braised with wine and spices, the sauce served with pasta, the meat as a main course.

## Sugoi

(Friuli-Venezia Giulia) Pork and cabbage soup.

## Sugoli

(Veneto) Grape jelly.

## Suino

Swine, pork.

## Sulcis

(Sardegna) *DOC* for dry red and rosé wines from the island of Sant'Antioco.

## Sultanine

Sultanas.

## Superiore

'Superior'. Having a higher degree of alcohol and sometimes longer ageing than the basic minimum, of some *DOC* wines.

## Supplì al telefono

(Lazio) Fried croquettes of rice stuffed with ham and *mozzarella* cheese, which melts to 'telephone wires'.

## Suricitti

(Marche) Fried maize flour dumplings with sausage.

## Surgelato

Frozen.

**Suro**
Scad, horse mackerel.

**Susamelli**
(Campania, Puglia) Sesame seed or almond and honey biscuits.

**Suspirus**
(Sardegna) Almond cakes.

**Svariati**
Assorted, various.

**Sylvaner**
White grape variety from the Rhine valley, grown on a small scale in the northeast.

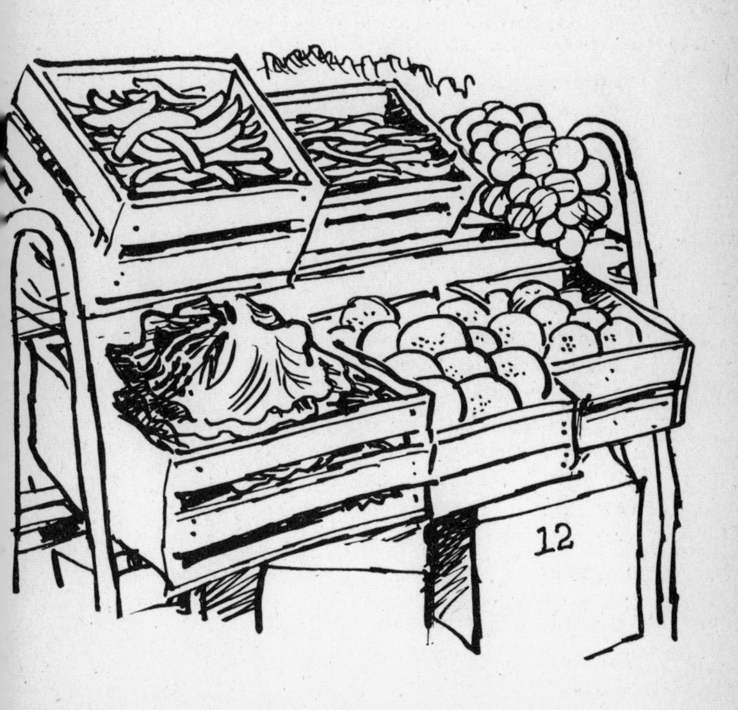

## Tacchino
Turkey. *T. alla canzanese in gelatina*: boned, rolled, served cold with white wine jelly.

## Tacconi
(Molise) Square pasta shapes, often with meat sauce.

## Taccula(s)
(Sardegna) Thrushes or blackbirds roasted, then kept in linen bags with myrtle leaves.

## Taggiaen
(Liguria) Green ribbon noodles, served with meat or mushroom sauce.

## Tagliarini
Thin pasta noodles, for soup.

## Tagliatelle/tagliatteli
(Emilia-Romagna) Long flat strips of egg pasta, slightly wider than *fettuccine*, traditionally accompanied by meat sauce. *T. alla biellese*: with milk, butter and parmesan. *T. della duchessa*: with chicken livers, egg yolks and parmesan; in honour of Marie-Louise of Austria. *T. alla romagnola*: with sausage, tomatoes and garlic.

## Tagliato
Cut, sliced.

## Taglierini
Thin pasta ribbons.

## (Da) Taglio
See *pesce*.

## Tagliolini
Very thin pasta noodles, for soup.

## Tajadale smalzade
(Trentino-Alto Adige) Thin pasta strands, with a sauce from veal stew.

## Tajarin
(Piemonte) Homemade thin pasta ribbons, usually served with butter, parmesan and truffles, or with chicken livers or meat sauce; also known as *ceresolini*.

## (Al) Tajo
See *risotto*.

## Taleggio
(Lombardia) Smooth cheese with fruity flavour.
*Taleggino*: stronger version.

## Tanuta
Black sea bream.

## Tapulòn (alla borgomanerese)
Stewed donkey or beef with red wine and cabbage.

### Taragna
See *polenta*.

### Taralli/taralucci
(Abruzzo, Puglia, Molise) Small spicy ring-shaped cakes.

### Tarant(i)ello
(Puglia, Calabria, Sicilia) Tuna fish sausage with spices.

### (Alla) Tarantina
In the style of Taranto, *Puglia*. See *ostriche*.

### Tardura
See *riso*.

### (Alla) Tartara
With tartare sauce.

### Tartaruga di mare
Turtle.

### Tarteletta
Tartlet.

### Tartina
Slice of bread spread with something.

### Tartufato
Truffled, with truffles.

### Tartufi
Truffles. *T. alla piemontese*: served with *bagna cauda* and garlic croûtons.
*Tartufato*: truffled, with truffles.
*Tartufi di mare/tartufoli*: Venus shells, type of small clam.

**Taurasi**
(Campania) Town known for magnificent red *DOC* wine based on *Aglianico* grapes.

**Tavola**
Table. *T. calda*: snack bar.

**Tazza**
Cup. *Tazzina*: small dish. *Nelle tazzine*: coddled, of eggs.

**Tè**
Tea.

**(In) Tecia**
(Veneto, Friuli-Venezia Giulia) Cooked, stewed, in an earthenware pot, of chicken, fish.

**(Alla) Tedesca**
German style. See *cavolo*.

**Tegame**
Heavy frying pan, skillet, casserole. *In/al tegame*: fried, pan- or pot-roasted.
*Al tegamino*: coddled, of eggs.

**Tegamaccio**
(Umbria) Rich stew of lake fish with oil, wine and herbs.

**Teglia**
Wide shallow baking dish.

**Tegol(in)e**
(Valle d'Aosta) Chocolate almond biscuits.

**(Al) Telefono**
See *suppli*.

**Telline**
Wedge-shells, small shellfish.

**Tempestine**
Tiny pasta shells, for soup.

**Tempia**
Head.

**Tenero**
Tender, soft, fresh.

**Teneroni (di vitello)**
Riblets, of veal.

**Tenuta**
Wine-growing estate, domaine.

**(Del) Teramano**
Of Teramo, *Abruzzo*. See *coratella, crespelle, minestrone*.

**Terlan(o)**
(Trentino-Alto Adige) *DOC* region known for light fresh white wines; 7 types permitted, 6 labelled according to grape variety, usually in German.

**(Alla) Ternana**
In the style of Terni, *Umbria*. See *ciriole, colombo, tortora*.

**Teroldego**
(Trentino-Alto Adige) Local grape variety. *T. rotaliano*: fine red *DOC* wine made from it.

**Terrina**
Terrine, pâté.

**Test(in)a/testarella**
Head. Cap, of mushroom. *Testa di puorco* (Sicilia): pig's head boiled with herbs, served cold. *Testina di vitello alla carniola*: boiled calf's head and brains, with herbs and horseradish sauce. *T. di v. alla toscana*: boiled, finished in oil with garlic and herbs.

**Testaroli/testetti**
(Liguria, Toscana) Wholemeal dumplings or rounds of yeast dough, served with *pesto* sauce.

**Testicoli**
Testicles. *Testicciuola di abbacchio* (Lazio): lamb's baked with garlic and herbs.

## (Al) Testo
See *pizza*.

## Testuggine marina
Turtle.

## Tiella
(Puglia, Lazio, Calabria) Large baking dish, and the food cooked in it – often layers of vegetables, or lamb's head and offal with potatoes, or mussels with potatoes and anchovies, or cheese and ham, sometimes in a pastry case.

## Tigella
(Emilia) Fried round of bread dough covered with bacon and herbs or cheese.

## Tignanello
(Toscana) Non-*DOC* red wine made by the famous *Chianti* house of *Antinori* from local grape varieties plus *Cabernet Sauvignon*; one of Italy's finest red wines.

## Timballo
Elaborate hot pie or mould. *T. all'abruzzese/timballe*: pancakes layered with meatballs, chicken giblets, cheese and tomato sauce, finished in the oven. *T. di maccheroni alla napoletana*: pastry pie filled with macaroni, chicken livers, mushrooms, cheese, served with meat sauce. *T. di m. alla pugliese*: macaroni, sausage, artichokes and cheese in a pastry case. *T. di riso alla piemontese*: rice mould with chicken livers, kidneys, meat sauce.

*Timballa e' latte* (Sardegna): baked almond custard; also known as *tumbàda*.

## Timo
Thyme, the herb.

## Timpano
(Campania) Baked slices of bread, sausage and cheese.

## Tinca
Tench, freshwater fish. *T. alla lariana*: sliced and stewed with onions and potatoes.

## Tira mi su
(Veneto) Rich sponge cake with cream, liqueur, chocolate and coffee.

## (Alla) Tirolese
In the style of the Tyrol, *Trentino-Alto Adige*. See *camoscio, knödel*.

## Tittoli
(Campania) Triangular *polenta* fritters.

## Tocai
White grape variety grown extensively in the north, with small amount of red *Tocai* also grown in *Veneto*.

## Toc de purcit
(Friuli-Venezia Giulia) Pork and liver stew with wine and spices.

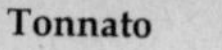

## (In) Tocchetti

See *burida.*

## Töcco

(Liguria) Meat or mushroom sauce, for pasta.

(Col) *tocco d'arrosto*: 'with a touch of the roast', i.e. leftover juices and meat.

## (Alla) Todina

In the style of Todi, *Umbria.* See *palombacce.*

## Tofeja canavesana

Pork offal, sausage and bean stew. See also *faseui.*

## Toma

(Piemonte) Smooth slightly holey firm yellow cheese.

## Tomaxelle

(Liguria) Veal rolls stuffed with mushrooms, pine nuts, cheese, braised in white wine, tomato and meat sauce.

## Tombarello

Frigate mackerel.

## Tomini

(Piemonte) Small round white cheeses, often of goat's milk with pepper.

## Tonco de pontesel

(Trentino-Alto Adige) Light veal stew.

## Tondino

(Puglia) Large round solid bread loaf.

## Tonnarelli

(Lazio) Very fine cut pasta strips, square in cross-section.

## Tonnato

With tuna or tuna sauce.

**Tonnellini**
Very thin match-like noodles.

**Tonn(ett)o/tonnino**
Tuna, tunny fish. *T. alla calabrese*: fried, with herbs, tomato and anchovy sauce. *T. alla contadina*: with wine, tomatoes and vinegar. *T. alla genovese*: slices stewed with anchovies, mushrooms, wine and spices. *T. fresco alla graela* (Veneto): slices marinated and grilled, with *polenta*. *T. alla siciliana*: with anchovies, herbs and wine.

**Topinambur**
Jerusalem artichoke.

**Topini**
(Puglia) Miniature *mozzarella* cheeses.

**Torbato**
(Sardegna) White grape variety, best known for *T. Secco di Alghero* made by *Sella & Mosca*.

**Torcalato**
(Veneto) Highly-regarded non-*DOC* sweet wine, made from semi-dried grapes in the *Breganze* area.

**Torcett(in)i**
(Piemonte, Valle d'Aosta) Light biscuits.

**Torcinelli**
(Abruzzo, Molise) Lamb's or goat's offal stuffed into an intestine and stewed; also known as *turcenelle, turcinelli*.

## Torciolo
Pancreas, of veal, beef.

## Torcolo
(Umbria) Ring-shaped cake with pine nuts, candied fruit, raisins, aniseed.

## Tordi
Thrushes. *T. in solea* (Puglia): poached with herbs and preserved in white wine.
Wrasse, sea fish.

## Torgiano
(Umbria) Red and white *DOC* wines; the red achieves international distribution under the Rubesco label.

## (Alla) Torinese
In the style of Turin, *Piemonte*. See *coppa, dolce, grissini, marmitta*.

## Torlo
Yolk, of egg.

## Torre Ercolana
(Lazio) Magnificent but rare non-*DOC* red wine.

## Torre Quarto
(Puglia) Wine made by the Cirillo-Farrusi family of Cerignola; the red has a specially good reputation.

## Torresani al spiedo
(Veneto) Pigeons wrapped in bacon, spit-roasted with spices.

## Torricelle
Horn-shells, cone-shaped shellfish.

## Torroncini
(Campania) Chocolate-coated biscuits.

## Torrone
Nougat. *T. gelato* (Calabria): almond and candied fruit log covered in chocolate. *T. molle*: chilled dessert of a biscuit and chocolate mixture.

## Torta
Cake, tart, pie, sweet or savoury. See also *pizza*. *T. fregolotti* (Trentino-Alto Adige, Veneto): 'fragile' almond cake with nuts; also known as *fregolatta*. *T. margherita*; basic sponge cake, often dusted with cocoa. *T. nera* (Emilia-Romagna): almond, chocolate and coffee cake. *T. di Orvieto*: cake with cherries, raisins, candied citron. *T. (del) paradiso* (Lombardia): rich cake served with cream. *T. pasqualina* (Liguria): pastry pie filled with greens and perhaps artichokes, curds and cheese. *T. salata di patate alla partenopea*: sausage and potato cake sprinkled with parmesan, baked. *T. sbricciolona/sbrisolana* (Lombardia): 'crumbly' almond cake.

## Tortel
(Trentino-Alto Adige) Baked potato tart.

## Tortelli

(Emilia-Romagna, Lombardia, Marche) Ravioli of various shapes and sizes, usually stuffed with spinach or chard, *ricotta* and other cheese. *T. alla cremasca*: stuffed with pounded macaroons, sultanas, nutmeg and cheese in a bow-shape, served with butter and cheese. *T. sguazzarotti*: stuffed with beans, pumpkin, nuts, served cold with a wine sauce. *T. di zucca*: stuffed with macaroon, pumpkin, pickled fruit and cheese.

## Tortellini

(Emilia-Romagna) Little rings of pasta with a stuffing. *T. alla bolognese*: filled with ham, pork and sausage. *T. all'emiliana*: stuffed with chicken, ham and truffle. *T. alla modenese*: with poultry and *ricotta* cheese filling.

## Tortelloni (alla romagnola)

Large pasta squares, stuffed with chard, or with *ricotta* and sage; also known as *turtlò*.

## Tortiera

Cake, pie.

*T. pugliese*: casserole of rice, potatoes, courgettes and peppers.

### Tortigliono
Almond cake.
*Tortiglioni*: spiral pasta shapes.

### Tortino
Thick flat omelette, often of vegetables. *T. alla toscana*: with tiny artichoke hearts.
Croquette, of cheese.
Pie, e.g. of pancakes layered with stuffing.

### Tortionata
(Lombardia) Crumbly almond cake.

### Tortore
Turtle doves. *T. alla ternana*: wrapped in ham and pastry, baked.

### (Alla) Toscana
In the style of *Toscana*. See *budino, castagnaccio, cetrioli, fagioli, frittelle, grillettato, minestrone, polpettone, risotto, roventini, testina, tortino, trippa*.

### Tosella
(Trentino-Alto Adige) Fried fresh cheese, served with *polenta*.

### Tostato
Toasted.

### Totano
Squid. *T. all' anacaprese*: preserved in oil and herbs.

### Tovaglia
Tablecloth. *Tovagliolo*: napkin.

### Tracine
Weevers, Mediterranean fish.

### Tramezzino
Sandwich. *Tramezzini* (Trentino-Alto Adige): slices of cold *polenta*, often with sausage.

### Traminer (Aromatico)
White grape variety grown in northeast; also known as *Gewurztraminer*.

### Trancia/trancio
Thick slice, e.g. of fish.

### Trani
(Puglia) Coastal port producing sweet white dessert wine *(DOC)* from *Moscato* grapes.

### (Alla) Trapanese
In the style of Trapani, *Sicilia*. See *ghiotta*.

### (Alla) Trappista
'Trappist monk's style'. See *fave*.

### (Del) Trasimeno
Of Lake Trasimeno, *Umbria*. See *luccio*.

### (Alla) Trasteverina
In the style of the Trastevere quarter of Rome, *Lazio*. See *animelle, baccalà, funghi, spezzatino, spinaci, trippa*.

### Trattalia
(Sardegna) Lamb's offal, bacon, bread wrapped in caul and spit-roasted or grilled.

### Trattoria
Small homely restaurant, tavern.

### Trebbianino Val Trebbia
(Emilia-Romagna) White *DOC* wine from a blend of grape varieties usually dry, sometimes sweet or semi-sparkling.

### Trebbiano
White grape variety grown throughout Italy, encountered in France as Ugni Blanc.

### Treccia
*Mozzarella* cheese, in a 'plait'.
(Abruzzo, Molise) Small bread loaf.

### Tregghi(ie)
Red mullet.

### Trenette
(Liguria) Narrow pasta strips, often served with *pesto* sauce, green beans and potatoes.

### (Alla) Trentina
In the style of Trento, *Trentino-Alto Adige*. See *anguilla, cuore, lepre, manzo, pollo, ravioli*.

### Trentino
Important wine growing area with 10 *DOC*'s named according to grape variety, centre of production for first-class sparkling wines.

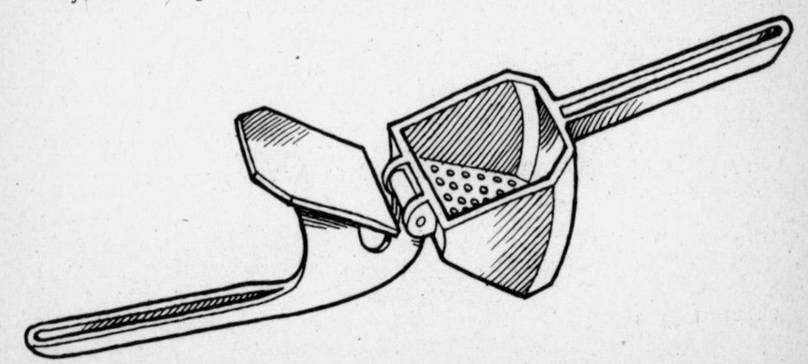

## (Alla) Trevigiana/trevisana

In the style of Treviso, *Veneto*. See *costicina, radicchio, risotto, trippa*.

## (Alla) Triestina

In the style of Trieste, *Friuli-Venezia Giulia*. See *fegato, granseola, patate, scaloppine*.

## Trifole

(Lombardia, Piemonte) Truffles.

*Trifolato*: sautéed with garlic and parsley, sometimes mushrooms and lemon, particularly of mushrooms, snails.

## Trigghie

(Sicilia) Red mullet.

## Trigli(ett)e (di scoglio)

Red mullet. *T. all'abruzzese/alla marina*: marinated and (charcoal) grilled. *T. alla napoletana*: grilled, with herbs and vinegar. *T. alla pugliese*: baked with herbs and garlic. *T. alla siciliana*: marinated and grilled, with orange. *T. alla veneziana*: fried, then marinated in white wine and served cold.

## Trigoli

(Lombardia) Water chestnuts.

## Trippa

Tripe. *T. alla bolognese/milanese*: with meat sauce and parmesan. *T. alla borghese*: simmered with mushrooms and garlic. *T. sottile alla fabrianese*: thin slices fried with mushrooms, and parmesan. *T. alla fiorentina/alla toscana*: simmered in tomato sauce with herbs, and parmesan at the end. *T. alla genovese*: stewed with mushrooms, pine nuts, meat sauce and wine; or with tomato sauce and potatoes, plus parmesan. *T. alla lucchese*: fried, sprinkled with cinnamon and parmesan. *T. alla manchigiana*: with bacon and tomato sauce, parmesan. *T. alla montanara/savoiarda*: poached in meat broth with onions, dressed with tomato sauce and spices. *T. alla napoletana*: finished with beaten egg and grated cheese. *T. all'olivitana*: baked with aubergines, eggs, cheese. *T. alla ragusana*: simmered in broth with aubergines, nuts, spices, plus cheese. *T. alla romana /alla trasteverina*: with a sauce of beef stew and mint. *T. alla trevisana*: with bacon and herbs, served on bread slices.

**Tritato**
Finely chopped, minced.

**Troccoli**
(Puglia) Thin square-cut pasta strips.

**Trof(f)ie**
(Liguria) Miniature dumplings or pasta spirals, often served with *pesto* sauce or cooked with potatoes and green beans.

**Trot(ell)a**
Trout. *T. alla savoia*: baked with mushrooms.
*Trota iridea*: rainbow trout.
*Trota salmonata*: salmon trout.

**Trun**
(Piemonte) Large type of fungus.

**Trunza di fera**
See *cavolo*.

**Tubellini/tubetti(ni)**
Tiny pasta tubes, for soup.

**Tufo**
(Campania) Small town with *DOC* for light, dry wines from *Greco* grapes.

**Tuma**
(Piemonte) Soft fat cheese.

**Tumbàd**
See *timballo*.

**Tuoni e lampo**
Pasta bits mixed with chick peas (like 'thunder and lightning').

**Tuorlo**
Yolk, of egg.

**Turbante**
Ring-shaped mould of food, often rice, with a filling in the centre.

**(Alla) Turca**
Turkish style. See *fave*.

**Turcenelle/turcinelli**
See *torcinelli*.

**Turchetti**
(Lazio) Small almond biscuits.

**Turdiddi**
(Calabria) Sweet fritters dipped in honey.

**Turta**

(Piemonte) Baked rice, spinach and cheese, sliced and eaten cold.
*Turta de faiscedda* (Sardegna): fried sweet cake of broad beans.

**Turtei**

(Lombardia) Pasta tubes. *T. sgrasaròt del baso mantovano*: stuffed with beans, grape must, jam and macaroons.

**Türteln**

(Trentino-Alto Adige) Rye ravioli stuffed with spinach and onion seeds.

**Turtiduzza**

(Sicilia) Fried lamb's or goat's offal, with tomato sauce.

**Turtlò**

See *tortelloni*.

**Tuvara dis arenas**

(Sardegna) Type of truffle found on seashore.

## Ua

(Veneto) Grapes.

## Uardi e fasui

(Friuli-Venezia Giuli) Barley, bean and ham bone soup.

## Ubriaco

See *maiale*.

## Uccelletti/uccellini

Small birds – thrushes, larks, figpeckers etc., usually roasted or grilled.

*Ucelletti di campagna/uccelli scappati*: beef olives, rolls, usually wrapped with ham slices, skewered and grilled.

*(All') uccelletto*: cooked like little birds, on skewers or with sage etc.

See also *fagioli, spiedini, vitella*.

## Ueta

(Veneto) Raisins.

## (All') Umberto di Savoia

See *costolette*.

## (All') Umbra

In the style of *Umbria*. With anchovy, tomato and truffle sauce, of pasta.
See also *broccoli, colombo, costolette, crostini, fette, pesce, zucchine*.

## Umbrici
(Umbria) Homemade spaghetti.

## (In) Umido
Stewed. Stew.

## Ungherese
Hungarian. See *salame*.

## Unicum
Proprietary aperitif bitters popular in the north.

## Uopa
(Sicilia) Bogue, type of sea bream.

## Uova
Eggs. *U. alla Bela Rosin* (Piemonte): egg mayonnaise; after the wife of Victor Emmanuel II. *U. filate*: ribbons of egg dough, added to clear soup. *U. fritte alla partenopea*: fried, with spaghetti, tomato sauce and cheese. *U. rotte all'acqua* (Sicilia): mixture of poached and beaten eggs, with cheese. *U. al tegame all altoatesina*: fried, with a slice of ham.

*Uovo di bufalo: mozzarella* cheese in an egg shape.

*Uova di tonno* (Sardegna): dried salted tuna roe. See also *limone*.

## (All') Uso
In the fashion of.

## Uva
Grapes. *U.passa/secca*: raisins. *U. sultanina/uvetta*: sultanas.

*Uva spina*: gooseberries.

**(Alla) Vaccinara**
See *coda*.

**Valcalepio**
(Lombardia) Small town producing fine red and white *DOC* wines.

**Valdadige**
(Trentino-Alto Adige) *DOC* zone making large quantities of red and white wine; also known as *Etschtaler*.

**Valdinievole**
(Toscana) *DOC* area producing dry white wine based on *Trebbiano* grapes.

**(Alla) Valdostana**
In the style of the *Valle d'Aosta*. See *caffè, camoscio, costolette, lessato, polenta*.

**(A la) Valesana**
See *mazaro*.

**Valgella**
See *Valtellina*.

**Valigini mantovani**
Cabbage rolls stuffed with chicken and potato, served with tomato sauce.

## Valle Isarco
(Trentino-Alto Adige) *DOC* region with 5 dry white wines authorized, named according to grape variety, usually in German; also known as *Eisacktaler*.

## Valpantena
Wine-growing district linked to *Valpolicella*.

## Valpolicella
(Veneto) 'Valley of many cellars'. *DOC* area celebrated for light dry red wine.

## Valtellina
(Lombardia) *DOC* region producing fine dry red wine based on *Nebbiolo* grapes; divided into 4 individual zones, *Sassella, Inferno, Grumello* and *Valgella*.

## Vapellinentze
Of the Valpelline, *Valle d'Aosta*. See *soupe*.

## (Della) Val Pusteria
Of the Val Pusteria, *Trentino-Alto Adige*. See *ravioli*.

## (Alla) Valtellinese
In the style of the Valtellina, *Lombardia*. See *risotto*.

## (Alla) Valusina
In the style of the Val de Susa, *Piemonte*. See *bistecca*.

## Vaniglia
Vanilla. *Vanigliato*: vanilla flavoured.

## Vassoio
Tray. Cheese board.

## Vasteddi
(Sicilia) Round bun filled with cheese and pork. See also *cavolfiore*.

## (Alla) Vastese
In the style of Vasto, *Abruzzo*. See *carpeselle, scapece*.

## (Alla) Vecchio maniera
Old-style.

## Vegetale
Vegetable.

## Velletri
(Lazio) Red and white *DOC* wines.

## Vellutata
Velouté soup.

## Vendemmia
Grape harvest. Vintage, of wine.

## Venegazzù
(Veneto) Wines made at Volpago del Montello by Conti Loredan; the Riserva della Casa, from Bordeaux grape varieties, is one of Italy's finest wines in the claret style.

## Venerdì Santo
Good Friday.

## (Alla) veneta
In the style of the *Veneto*. See *frittata, frittura, polenta, zucchine*.
Round bread loaf.

## (Alla) Veneziana
In the style of Venice, *Veneto*. See *anguilla, carciofi, cavolo, fegato, granseola, ostriche, patate, riso, rognoni, scampi, seppie, sogliola, triglie*.

## Ventaglio
Scallop, shellfish.
*A ventaglio*: fan-shaped.

## Ventresca
Stomach, belly of tuna fish, pork.

## Ventricina
(Abruzzo) Spicy pork sausage.

## Verace
Authentic, true. Fresh, not tinned.

## Verbesco
(Piemonte) Branded dry white wine made from red *Barbera* grapes fermented without contact with the skins.

## (Alla) Vercellese
In the style of Vercelli, *Piemonte*. See *rane*.

## Verde
Green. With spinach, of pasta. *Al verde*: with herbs or vegetables.

## Verdesca
Shark.

## Verdicchio
(Marche) White grape variety.

## Verdure
Vegetables.

## Verduzzo
White grape variety grown in the northeast.

## Vermentino
Grape variety both red and white.

## Vermicelli(ni)
Thin pasta strands; the usual southern name for spaghetti. *V. atterati* (Campania): with butter, pine nuts and chocolate. *V. alla sammartinese* (Calabria): with bacon and hot pepper.

## Vermouth
Wine-based aperitif flavoured with herbs and spices, generally with strong brand image, e.g. *Martini, Cinzano*; said to have originated commercially in Turin, *Piemonte*.

## Vernaccia
Group of grape varieties; the name is applied in many areas to wines that are not necessarily related.

## Vernatsch
See *Schiava.*

## Vero
Real, authentic.

## (Alla) Veronese
In the style of Verona, *Veneto*. See *macaroni, radicchio, risotto, sedano.*

## Verrùch
(Puglia) Turnip-type vegetable, used in salad.

## Verza
Savoy cabbage. *Verzata alla milanese*: cabbage and pork soup.

## Verzelata
Grey mullet.

## Verzini
Small cooking sausages.

## Vescica
Bladder.

## Vespolina
(Piemonte) Red grape variety.

## Vezzena

(Veneto) Smooth fairly fat cheese.

## Viccillo

(Campania) Ring-shaped yeast pastry filled with egg, sausage and cheese.

## (Alla) Vicentina

In the style of Vicenza, *Veneto*. See *baccalà, fegato, stinco, stoccafisso.*

## Vigna/vigneto

Vineyard.

## Vignaiolo

Grape farmer.

## (Alla) Vignarola

'Wine-grower's style'. See *lepre.*

## (Alla) Villana

'Rustic' style.

## Vin

Wine.

*Vin Cotto*: 'cooked wine'. Wine made from grape juice reduced by boiling, usually strong and sweet.

*Vin Santo*: 'holy wine'. Wine made from semi-dried grapes with long slow fermentation and many years ageing; may be dry or sweet, with some similarity to sherry, but not fortified.

## Vincisgrassi

(Marche, Abruzzo) Pasta sheets layered with butter, cream, ham, chicken livers and truffles, after the Austrian, Prince Windischgratz; also known as *pincisgrassi.*

## Vinello

Light quaffing wine.

## Vino

Wine. Throughout Italy – Enotria or 'land of wine' as it was known to the ancients – the vine grows naturally in hundreds of different varieties and wine used to be a normal part of every farmer's harvest, mostly for personal or local consumption. In 1963 *DOC* was enacted to control this vast production, to encourage commercial exploitation and to preserve the individuality of the best of countless local wines, resulting in (at present) over 200 specified *DOC* areas, making about 500 wines. However, this represents only about 14% of the total, the rest being table wine. *DOC* regulations cover most aspects of the production of a wine, and its principal definitions concern territory and grape variety. This is reflected in the names or appellations which are roughly divided into two groups – one, the older group, named simply after place of origin (as are most wines in France), e.g. *Soave, Frascati, Orvieto;* the other named by grape variety allied to a place name, e.g. *Barbera d'Alba, Cortese di Gavi, Alto Adige Merlot. DOCG* is a higher category of the elite. It is important to note that, although *DOC* was designed to emphasize

ANNATA
1980
Vintage.
Year of production.
VILLA CERNA
CHIANTI CLASSICO
DENOMINAZIONE DI ORIGINE CONTROLLATA
IMBOTTIGLIATO ALL'ORIGINE
NELL'AZIENDA AGRARIA DI VILLA CERNA s.a.s
CERNA-CASTELLINA IN CHIANTI-ITALIA
0.750 LITRI e
R.I. 372/SI
12% VOL
Name of estate.
Category D.O.C.
Estate bottled by
Name of grower/bottler
Alcohol conten
Contents.
E.E.C approved size.
Official number of bottler.
Address of grower/bottler
Area of origin Chianti. Classico indicates central vineyard ar

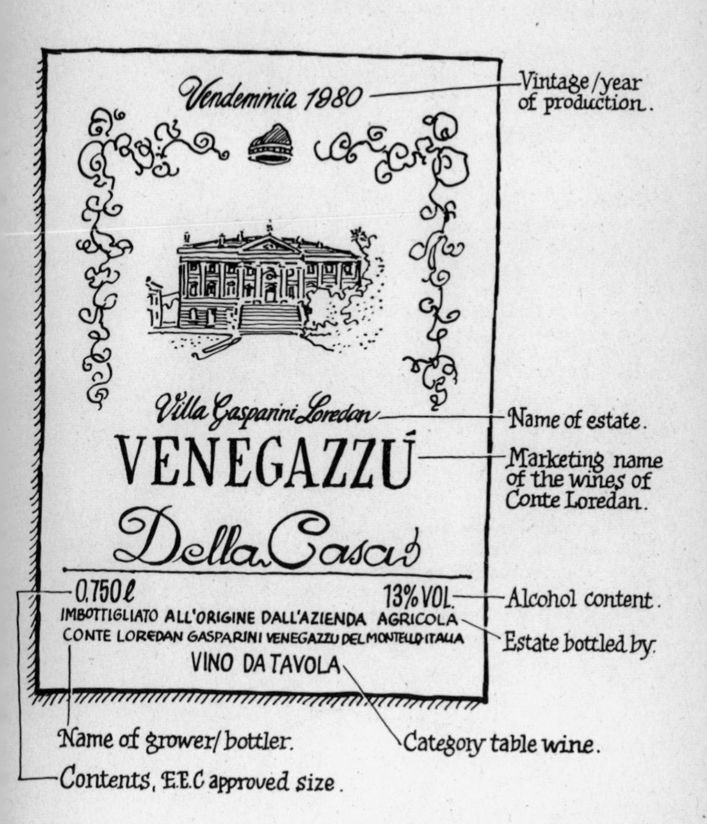
Vendemmia 1980
Villa Gasparini Loredan
VENEGAZZÚ
Della Casa
0,750 ℓ
13% VOL.
IMBOTTIGLIATO ALL'ORIGINE DALL'AZIENDA AGRICOLA
CONTE LOREDAN GASPARINI VENEGAZZU DEL MONTELLO ITALIA
VINO DA TAVOLA
Vintage/year of production.
Name of estate.
Marketing name of the wines of Conte Loredan.
Alcohol content.
Estate bottled by.
Name of grower/bottler.
Category table wine.
Contents, E.E.C approved size.

quality, many of Italy's finest wines do not claim the classification and are rated merely as table wines, e.g. *Sassicaia, Tignanello, Spanna*. For this reason the reputation of the grower or estate is often more important than the official classification of the wine.

*V. novello*: 'new wine' made to be ready for drinking before Christmas of the year of harvest; equivalent to French 'nouveau'.

*V. da pasta*: ordinary table wine.

*V. da tavola*: table wine sometimes 'con indicazione geografica', with identification of a place name. EEC category for all wines that are not *VQPRD*.

*V. tipico*: EEC category for wine typical of specific areas; not yet introduced into Italy it will constitute a class between *vino da tavola* and *DOC*.

## (Alla) Violetta

With candied violets.

## Violini

(Lombardia) Salted smoked goat meat (sliced with the movement of a violin bow). See also *pesce*.

## Virtù

(Abruzzo) Thick vegetable and meat soup (made with 7 types of ingredient and cooked for 7 hours).

## Vite

Vine.

## Vitellini

See *ciciones*.

## Vitello

Veal, technically the meat of milk-fed calves. *V. di latte*: sucking calf. *V.alla genovese*: thin slices with wine and artichokes. *V. alla sarda*: larded with anchovies, braised, with tomatoes and olives. *V. tonnato*: (Piemonte, Lombardia): cold roast or boiled, with tuna, anchovy and caper sauce. *V. all'uccelletto* (Liguria): slices sautéed with herbs and white wine.

*Vitello di mare* (Veneto): dogfish, shark.

**Vitellone**
Young beef, up to 3 years old.

**Viticoltore**
Grape farmer.

**Vittoria**
(Sicilia) *Cerasuolo di V.*: strong dry rosé wine *(DOC)*, often aged for many years in wood; also known as *Frappato*.

**Volante**
See *pesce*.

**Vongole**
Carpet-shells, small clams.

**VQPRD**
'Vini di Qualità Prodotti in Regione Delimitate', EEC classification for quality wines produced in a defined region; also applies to sparkling wines – VSQPRD.

**VSQPRD**
See *VQPRD*.

**V(u)opa**
(Sicilia) Bogue, type of sea bream.

**Vulture**
(Basilicata) *DOC* zone for strong red wine made from *Aglianico* grapes, sometimes sparkling.

## Weissburgunder
See *Pinot*.

## Welschriesling
See *Riesling*.

## Würstel
(Trentino-Alto Adige) Frankfurter sausage.

## Zabaione/zabaglione
(Piemonte) Frothy mixture of egg yolks and Marsala, served warm as a dessert; or made with white wine and without sugar as a savoury sauce.

## Zafferano
Saffron.

## Zagarlo
(Lazio) Small town, producing dry and semi-sweet white *DOC* wine.

## Zaleti/Zalett
(Veneto, Emilia-Romagna) Yellow sultana biscuits.

## Zampe
Feet, trotters.

## Zampetto
Pig's leg.

## Zampone
(Emilia-Romagna) Creamy fresh pork sausage, packed into a pig's leg, usually boiled and served hot with lentils, potatoes or other boiled meats.

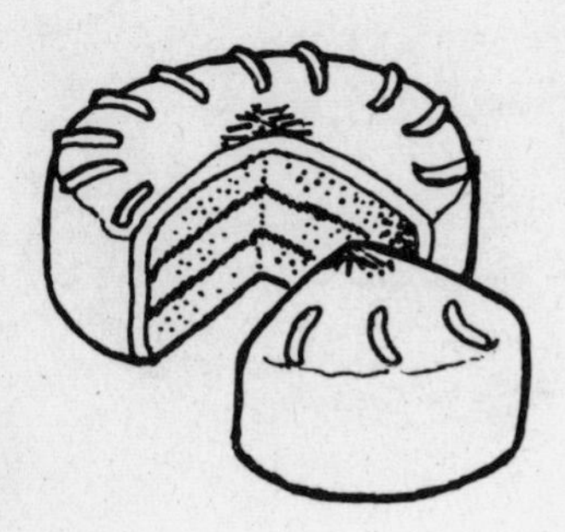

## (Alla) Zappatora
'Peasant's style'. (Puglia) With garlic and hot pepper, of pasta.

## Zastoch
(Friuli-Venezia Giulia) Fried beans, potato and pumpkin.

## Zelten
(Trentino-Alto Adige) Rye cake with dried fruits, nuts, honey.

## Zembi d'arzillo
(Liguria) Ravioli with a fish filling.

## Zenzero
Ginger.
(Toscana) Hot red pepper.

## Zeppole
(Campania, Calabria, Abruzzo) Sweet fritters, sometimes with chestnuts and chocolate.

## Zermegai
See *fagioli*.

## Zerri
Picarel, sea fish.

## Zesti
(Piemonte) Candied orange and lemon peel.

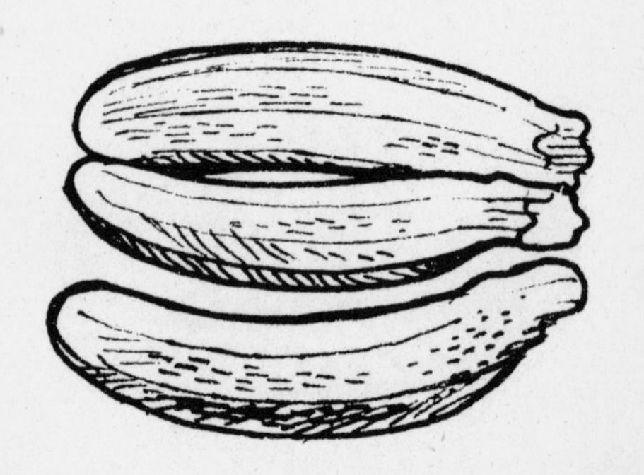

## (Alla) Zia
'Aunt's style'. Indicating a homely preparation.

## Zibidina
(Friuli-Venezia Giulia) Jellied pork brawn.

## (In) Zimino/ziminu
(Liguria, Sardegna) Stewed, especially of squid or cuttlefish with spinach and herbs, or of snails. Soup, e.g. of chick peas.

**Zippulas**
(Sardegna) Honey fritters.

**Zita/zite/zit(on)i**
Large thick macaroni. *Zite ripiene alla casertana*: stuffed with pork sausage, spices and cheese and finished in the oven. Z. *alla napoletana*: with a rich beef, ham and wine sauce, tomatoes and pine nuts.

**Zonin**
(Veneto) Major producer and shipper of wines.

**Zucca**
Pumpkin. Z. *alla fiorentina*: filled with cream and butter and baked.

**Zuccarini**
(Sicilia) Sweet biscuits.

**Zucchero**
Sugar.
*Zuccheri*: sugar content on wine labels.
*Zuccherini di Bettona*: sweet pastry rings with nuts and raisins.

**Zuchette zucchine**
Courgettes, zucchini. Z. *al tegame alla romana/all'umbra*: stewed with oil, onion, tomatoes. Z. *alla veneta*: fried with beaten egg as an omelette.

**Zuccotto**
(Toscana) Dome-shaped cake with liqueurs, chocolate, cream and nuts.

**Zuf**
(Friuli-Venezia Giulia) Hot *polenta* porridge, served with milk.

## Zuppa

Thick soup poured over slices of bread or containing bread. Z. *acida alla bolzanese*: tripe soup with cream, lemon, sauerkraut, served with *polenta*. Z. *alla canàvesana*: layered cabbage, bread, sausage, cheese, with broth, browned in the oven. Z. *cuata* (Sardegna): of meat, cheese, bread. Z. *mitonà* (Piemonte): broth poured over garlic toast. Z. *pavese*: clear soup with poached egg, fried bread and cheese. Z. *di pesce*: fish soup, stew, with many local versions. Z. *del povero*: broccoli or other greens, with bread. Z. *sarda*: broth with beaten egg and cheeses. Z. *scaligera* (Veneto): pigeon, turkey, cheese layered with bread, plus broth, finished in the oven; after the Scala family, rulers of Verona. Z. *di soffrito* (Campania): of pig's offal and tomato, served with bread or spaghetti. See also *acquacotta*, *ghiotta*.

*Zuppa inglese* (Emilia-Romagna): sponge cake soaked in liqueur and layered with custard.

## Zurrette

(Sardegna) Cooked lamb's or goat's blood and cheese, served cold or grilled.